THE SPIRIT OF
JAPANESE CAPITALISM
AND SELECTED ESSAYS

THE SPIRIT OF
JAPANESE CAPITALISM
AND SELECTED ESSAYS

Yamamoto Shichihei

Translated by
Lynne E. Riggs and Takechi Manabu

Introduction by
Frank Gibney

MADISON BOOKS
Lanham • New York • London

Published by Madison Books
4720 Boston Way
Lanham, Maryland 20706

3 Henrietta Street
London WC2E 8LU England

Co-published by arrangement with the Pacific Basin
Institute

Distributed by National Book Network

The Library of Japan Edition First Published April
1992.

The paper used in this publication meets the minimum
requirements of American National Standard for
Information Sciences—Permanence of Paper for
Printed Library Materials, ANSI Z39.48–1984. ∞™
Manufactured in the United States of America.

Library of Congress Cataloging-in-Publication Data

Yamamoto, Shichihei, 1921–
The spirit of Japanese capitalism and selected essays /
Yamamoto Shichihei ; translated by Lynne E. Riggs
and Takechi Manabu ; introduction by Frank
Gibney.
p. cm. – (Library of Japan)
1. Capitalism—Japan. I. Title. II. Series.
HC462.9.Y2545 1992
330.12'2'0952—dc20 91–43856 CIP

ISBN 0–8191–8294–X (cloth : alk. paper)

British Cataloging in Publication Information Available

Partial funding provided by The Japan Foundation and
the Japan–United States Friendship Commission.

CONTENTS

INTRODUCTION

In 1970 a memorable book appeared in Tokyo called *The Japanese and the Jews*. Written in Japanese—and very well written—it purported to be a comparison of the Jews and the Japanese, as specially endowed peoples. In point of fact, it was an attempt to produce a dispassionate evaluation of the modern Japanese, as they are now, from a friendly but coolly objective quarter. The book, which sold 2,500,000 copies in Japan, was later translated into English. After a few years, however, its pseudonymous author, one Isaiah Ben Dasan, was revealed to be in reality Yamamoto Shichihei, a Japanese publisher and occasional essayist, who until that point had written very little.*

In the years since then, Yamamoto wrote a great deal. After *The Japanese and the Jews* was finished, he followed with his wartime reminiscences. Titled *A Low Ranking Officer in the Imperial Army*, it constitutes an intuitive, often brilliantly written series of autobiographical notes about the Japanese defeat in the Pacific War. Ex-Lieutenant Yamamoto had served in an artillery regiment on Luzon until

---

*Interestingly enough, those who read the English-language version first immediately recognized that the author was Japanese. On the other hand, the structural vagueness of Japanese left a reader wondering whether Isaiah Ben Dasan wasn't a real person after all. At least the Japanese version fooled me, when I read it.

his capture by U.S. forces late in 1944. In the course of recounting his own experience, he makes some fascinating comments on the entire Japanese military effort and its origins.

His perspective is an interesting one. Yamamoto was accepted in the volunteer officer training corps after graduating from Aoyama Gakuin University. As a third-generation Christian and a believing one—a rarity in Japanese life—he was able to look quite dispassionately at the Japanese military institution in World War II.

Some years thereafter, Yamamoto wrote the book we now present in translation: *The Spirit of Japanese Capitalism.* In this volume he sets out to analyze the background of the Japanese business society, including its origins, which he traces back before the Meiji Restoration to the Tokugawa period of seclusion in the seventeenth and eighteenth centuries.

It is interesting to note that the author's emphasis differs from most current explanations of Japan's postwar business success. There is very little about the U.S. Occupation or the prodigies performed by the Ministry of International Trade and Industry and other wings of Japan's business-minded bureaucracy. There are no thumbnail sketches of Sony or Matsushita in action. Rather, Yamamoto has gone back to the past to seek out some basic cultural and historical roots which explain why Japanese businessmen behave the way they do. His historical study goes beyond the Meiji Restoration, Japan's striking self-modernization in 1868, and looks at the two hundred-fifty-odd years of seclusion before that time.

It was during this time, in the Tokugawa shogunate, that the Japanese developed many of their modern, national traits and reflexes in relative isolation. Yamamoto brings all this out. He shows how the Japanese view toward business contracts, for example, is deeply rooted in Japan's past—not something that just developed over the postwar period because of an aversion to reading fine print in western languages. He goes back to the Japanese Buddhist and Confucian ethic to trace the origins of the modern work ethic. It is not too much to say that what Max Weber in his memorable writings did for the European Protestant ethic, Yamamoto has done for the Japanese. His is a unique approach to explaining Japan's modern business successes.

Yamamoto's keen analyses have won him a tremendous reputation as a business writer and theorist in Japan. Since writing *The Spirit of Japanese Capitalism,* he has gone on to write a series of books on similar subjects. He contributes to various monthly and weekly magazines, including a frequently found column in *Nikkei Business,* Japan's tremendously successful economic journal, and has lectured widely on Japanese business practices throughout the world.

In recent years he has expanded his focus to discuss, once again, the singularities of Japanese society and Japan's peculiar position in the modern world. It would require little exaggeration to think of Yamamoto as a latter-day Fukuzawa Yukichi in reverse. Fukuzawa, the great modernizer of the nineteenth century, explained the Western world to his readers in Japan. Similarly Yamamoto has set out to explain the modern Japanese to the world around them, a world in which they now play such a major economic role.

I have known Yamamoto for many years and have found him a graceful, stimulating and fair-minded social critic, in the best sense of the word. He is also a good friend, whose quiet wit and deep knowledge make him a pleasure to associate with.

Despite the wide dissemination of his writing in Japanese, this marks the first time any of his business writings have been translated into English in book form. I consider it essential reading for a complete understanding of Japan's modern business society, how it grew and where it may be going.

THE SPIRIT OF
JAPANESE CAPITALISM

1

A PROTESTANT ETHIC IN A NON-CHRISTIAN CONTEXT

For you yourselves know how you ought to imitate us; we were not idle when we were with you, we did not eat anyone's bread without paying. . . . For even when we were with you, we gave you this command: If any one will not work, let him not eat. For we hear that some of you are living in idleness, mere busy bodies, not doing any work. Now such persons we command and exhort in the Lord Jesus Christ to do their work in quietness and to earn their own living. (II Thess. 3: 7–12)

All occupations are Buddhist practice; through work we are able to attain Buddhahood. There is no calling that is not Buddhist. All is for the good of the world. . . . The all-encompassing Buddha-nature manifest in us all works for the world's good: without artisans, such as the blacksmith, there would be no tools; without officials there would be no order in the world; without farmers there would be no food; without merchants we would suffer inconvenience. All the other occupations as well are for the good of the world. . . . All reveal the blessing of the Buddha. Those who are ignorant of the blessing of our Buddha-nature, who do not value themselves and their innate Buddha-nature and fall into evil ways of thinking and behaving, have lost their way. (Suzuki Shōsan, *Shimin nichiyō*)

Not leisure and enjoyment, but only activity serves to increase the glory of God, according to the definite manifestations of His will. . . . For, in conformity with the Old Testament and in analogy to the ethical valuation of good works, asceticism looked upon the pursuit of wealth as an end in itself as highly reprehensible; but the attainment of it as a fruit of labour in a calling was a sign of God's blessing. And even more important: the religious valuation of restless, continuous, systematic work in a worldly calling, as the highest means to asceticism, and at the same time the surest and most evident proof of rebirth and genuine faith, must have been the most powerful conceivable lever for the expansion of that attitude toward life which we have here called the spirit of capitalism.

When the limitation of consumption is combined with this release of acquisitive activity, the inevitable practical result is obvious: accumulation of capital through ascetic compulsion to save. (Max Weber, *The Protestant Ethic and the Spirit of Capitalism*)

It is perhaps unusual to begin an essay with three quotations, but all of the above illuminate a core aspect of the phenomenon we are concerned with in this book—Japanese capitalism. The often-quoted passage from Thessalonians should be familiar, and many readers know the work of Max Weber, yet few perhaps have ever heard of the Zen monk Suzuki Shōsan (1579–1655). What is interesting about Suzuki, as we shall see, is that the ideas he articulated have had an impact in Japan comparable to the effect of the Protestant ethic, as Max Weber analyzed it, in the West.

Historically, Japan is one of the few countries in the world that have not been influenced to some degree by the Bible. In this respect, Japan is further away from the West than are the Islamic nations, China, or India; the cultural distance, indeed, removes Japan to the "very far" East. Japanese of a century ago knew nothing of the Protestant ethic, out of which, according to Weber, the ethos of capitalism was formed.

But Japan did, without the help of the Bible, develop a capitalistic system so successful that foreign missions from all over the world come to see how it works. Most of them leave feeling that they still don't fully understand its essence. Numerous studies on Japan's economic system have been published abroad, yet few so far have clearly delineated the spiritual "something" that underlies capitalism in Japan, or anything comparable to the Protestant ethic that is the spiritual basis of Western capitalism.

Japan's successful modernization has been variously attributed to a miracle, a genius for imitation, luck. But in this day and age there are no miracles, and Western civilization can hardly be so simple as to lend itself to wholesale imitation. Finally, how "lucky" are the Japanese, who in this century alone have survived the Great Kantō Earthquake of 1923, which devastated Tokyo, the destruction of nearly all our large cities in World War II, and, on top of that, the horror of the atomic bomb? On more than one occasion the Japanese people have felt truly forsaken by the Goddess of Fortune. It is not luck or genius in copying, it is something else that has propelled Japan's progress. I do not believe that Western observers have necessarily *overlooked* that "something" underlying capitalism in Japan. Instead, because of the language barrier and other factors, they have been unable to see it.

In this book we will discuss that "something," using material that appears for the first time in English. But we should remember at the outset that just as John Calvin did not consciously set about to build the spiritual foundation for capitalism, neither did the austere Zen monk Suzuki Shōsan.

Suzuki labels greed—what Weber calls "the pursuit of wealth"—a spiritual poison. But at the same time he says, "All occupations are Buddhist practice; through work we are able to attain Buddhahood." Suzuki considers worldly labor a form of ascetic Zen exercise that can help one attain Buddhahood (salvation). To immerse oneself in work is "the surest and most evident proof of rebirth and genuine faith." This thinking, like the Protestant ethic, has led to the equation of thrift with secular asceticism.

In both cases, this became the spiritual ethos at the base of capitalism, and it continues to provide norms for social behavior. Any attempt to study a country without taking into consideration the history of such ideas is certain to breed misunderstandings. It is my sincere hope that this book will help in some measure to avoid such misunderstandings in the future.

Unseen Principles

We must be careful when we speak of capitalism. Once we label a system "capitalist," we assume that it possesses all the characteristics associated with the word. It is all too easy to assume that because Japan and the United States are both capitalistic countries they have the same economic systems, and that research on and analysis of the American system and the policies that have been formulated for it are equally applicable in Japan. As we shall see, this is hardly the case.

I once attended a meeting at which a prominent economist spoke on the Japanese economy. As I listened I began to feel uneasy: It seemed to me that the "capitalism" he was analyzing, criticizing, and formulating policies for did not exist in Japan. I saw our system as something altogether different, and it seemed that the policies he was proposing could be applied only to the imaginary system he had conjured up in his speech. Was it not possible, I asked myself, that the Japanese economy functioned on its own, unseen principles? If so, what were they? Aware that I risked offending, I nevertheless put to him the following question:

As the owner of a tiny publishing house, I am one of Japan's many small businessmen.* All my business dealings are with

---

*Definitions of small and medium-sized enterprises in Japan vary widely and are

4

other small businessmen. Even the largest of book distributors does far less business than one section of a large trading house (*sōgō shōsha*). What you've been discussing is totally irrelevant to us small businessmen. As you know, more than 95 percent of all businesses in Japan are small or medium-sized and they employ about 80 percent of all workers. If the capitalism you've just described exists at all in Japan, it involves only a fraction of all our companies and employees. I wonder if one can ever hope to make a meaningful analysis of the Japanese economy without taking into consideration the overwhelming majority of businesses and workers?

Because I knew the speaker to be highly opinionated, I braced myself for a spirited rebuttal. Instead, after a prolonged silence, he replied, "I do not wish to comment on your question."

No doubt my question was inappropriate at such a gathering, where everyone is expected to play intellectual games. It was definitely bad form to challenge the premise on which the game was based. Hence the awkward silence that fell over the room.

Finally, someone spoke up in the speaker's defense. "Perhaps what we're discussing accounts for only 5 and 20 percent of the whole; but inasmuch as they dominate the economy, whatever principles apply to them cannot be considered irrelevant to the rest." To his mind, the economist's imaginary capitalism existed in Japan. I returned,

Yes, but if small-to-medium-sized businesses indeed ran on different principles, then we smaller businessmen would experience the

---

extremely complex. The Basic Law on Small and Medium-sized Enterprises defines such companies as follows: (1) a mining or manufacturing enterprise which is capitalized at no more than 100 million yen and that regularly employs less than three hundred people; (2) a wholesaler with less than thirty million yen and a hundred employees; (3) a retail establishment that has less than 10 million yen in capital and fifty employees.

same difficulties in our dealings with large Japanese corporations that we experience when we do business with American firms. Most of us are subcontractors, yet in our dealings with parent companies we do *not* experience such problems. I simply cannot believe that we operate on different principles.

Once again a chill fell over the group. I knew that I was breaking all the rules of etiquette, but I was not arguing for the sake of argument, nor was I taking the speaker to task for his views. I sincerely wanted him to enlighten me about the norms—those unseen principles—that actually govern Japanese companies, large and small alike.

The Protestant Ethic

The outward forms of capitalism have spread throughout the world. But it does not necessarily follow that when outward forms are the same, internal systems also work the same way. Take the capitalistic practices of overseas Chinese merchants; they had little to do with the Protestant ethic as Max Weber describes it. Any theory that tried to relate the Protestant ethic and the capitalism of overseas Chinese would only prove that there was no connection whatsoever. Were one to search for the unseen guiding principles of economics in the Chinese merchant community, one would have to look to Chinese tradition. The same may be said about the Middle East. Knowing some Palestinian "capitalists," I can say with confidence that the norms they follow bear no resemblance to those of either Westerners or Japanese, and I am sure that their norms differ from those of overseas Chinese merchants as well.

Such differences are only natural. After all, societies have distinct social structures based on unique traditions. Each operates according to its own principles, reflecting the attitudinal and behavioral patterns of its members. Although enterprises in these countries share certain outward features of capitalism, their modes of operation differ from one culture to another. While the principles by which they operate may be invisible to those outside the culture, they are self-evident to those within—everyone knows exactly what they are. In Japan, however, no one talks about them. Just as it would be meaningless to study the capitalism of Chinese merchants without taking their culture into consideration, we must also examine Japanese culture if we wish to unravel the hidden principles behind capitalism in our country. The problem is that in our case we are not supposed to discuss them, as my experience at the meeting shows. This is another "hidden principle." But as long as we avoid discussing the unseen principles that govern our corporate and individual behavior, we will never be able to clarify, much less solve, problems confronting our economy.

The Japanese propensity for keeping these unseen principles out of all formal discussion is not limited to economics; it permeates the whole society. In politics we imported our parliamentary system from the West, but because we did not import parliamentarians or the electorate, we can never expect our system to function in the same way as Western systems. Even children can see that the systems do not function in the same way, as a glance at the Letters to the Editor section of any newspaper will show. There, fourteen- or fifteen-year-olds develop hard-and-fast arguments criticizing the extent to which our political system deviates from the Western model. But no number of letters is of any use when the writers themselves are controlled by a set of unseen principles. We use imported criteria in criticizing others, while we follow indigenous, informal norms in our own behavior. Yet we are not supposed to blame each other for this dualism. This is still another "unseen principle."

I cannot take up all manifestations of the hidden principles in Japanese society in this book. I shall limit my discussion to their economic implications. I began my discussion with small and medium-sized businesses because they are the most typical of economic organizations functioning according to principles that defy all scholarly theories. Yet those principles have their own rationality, and anyone who ignores them will not get very far in business.

Needless to say, I am not an outside observer, nor am I a specialist on the economics of small business. I was over fifty when I began my career as a writer. For a long time I was just an employee at a small publishing house until at last I managed to establish my own company. I have seen how the world of small business simply abounds with mysterious phenomena that seem to have no rational explanation. Though miles apart from scientific analysis and the world of learning, Japan's small businesses were, in the long run, directly responsible for the recovery and growth of the Japanese economy, which way outstripped all forecasts made in the early post-World War II years. Japan's economic miracle was but the sum of the irrational phenomena in the world of small business. Let me elaborate on this point by describing some of the printers and binders I know.

Empty Theory versus the Wisdom of Experience

Most people who own or manage small businesses do not possess impressive academic credentials. The printers and binders I know have not studied Marxian or Keynesian economics, or modern principles of management. Even the word "management" acquired meaning for them only during the period of rapid growth in the 1960s. Most founded their companies themselves or else started from scratch after the war to rebuild family businesses, virtually all of which had been destroyed by America's devastating bombing raids. Half of these men were born around 1920; they received no college education before the war, nor were they affected by the postwar educational reform. With experience as their teacher and observation as their text, they learned the structure of society, the psychology of its members, and how to apply their knowledge in the real world. In the process they evolved a set of norms by which to conduct their business.

Be that as it may, these small businessmen never thought of entering into productive debate with prominent economists over the capitalism they practiced. They knew very well that the wisdom of their experience would not mesh with scholarly theories. Unable to put their experience into words, they could not even discuss it among themselves, much less theorize about it. One might say they suffered from a form of aphasia, and, as a consequence, developed a love-hate relationship with anything academic or abstract. While they were outwardly respectful toward scholarly theory, inwardly they dismissed it as meaningless. Formal learning to them was a sort of play acted out on an intellectual stage, subject to its own rules. Although they might be able to glean something useful from it— and they had a tremendous thirst for knowledge—it was certainly not applicable per se in the real world. Had one of their number applied such theories to his business and gone bankrupt, they would have had nothing but contempt for him. To them, he would have been trying to live a life portrayed on stage. The kindest thing they could have said about him would be, "He should have been a scholar."

During my thirty years in the publishing world, I have seen a good many companies go bankrupt, including the foremost prewar publisher, Kaizōsha, and the oldest publishing house with a history spanning more than four generations, Uchida Rōkakuho. What is significant about the demise of these two giant publishing houses is that in both cases their presidents went to the United States shortly after World War II, where they studied economics and management. On their return to Japan, they applied what they had learned.

Of the two publishing houses, Kaizōsha is gone for good, now all but forgotten, while Uchida Rōkakuho has been reborn. Because I know the people there very well, I was able to learn the inside story, which was an incredible one. When the senior manager, who had risen through the ranks under the president's father, and other employees realized that the company's end was near, they staged a coup d'état with the creditors' support, and ousted the president. The senior manager was appointed president, they incorporated and made the creditors their stockholders, and soon they had the company on its feet again.

This company has since prospered simply on the empirical wisdom of its new president. It is tempting to say that had the U.S.-educated president left the operation of the company to this experienced manager, he would not have had to be removed. The uneducated manager learned the spirit of Japanese capitalism through experience. He knows nothing of economics or management theory, but he has a firm grasp of unseen principles.

Because he could not put these principles into words, however, he could not argue with the young president over his American ideas of management. The manager had no choice but to keep silent and wait. Underlying his attitude was the firm conviction that, whether or not he could stand up to the president in a contest of words, his approach would no doubt prove itself superior in actual practice. Extremely competent as a manager, yet weak in theoretical argument, he is typical of the sort of man who stood behind Japan's phenomenal economic growth.

Extracontractual Relationships

On more than one occasion I have found myself perplexed by questions involving the unseen principles operative in Japanese society. Once a Western businessman who knows Japan well asked me, "Japan supposedly has a lifelong employment system; what sort of contracts do you sign?" I could not give him any plausible answer offhand. Indeed, employment in Japan is generally for life, but we sign no contract to that effect when we enter a company. Every Japanese knows the unwritten rule that if he were to demand such a contract he would not be hired in the first place, or that the company would reverse its decision to employ him before he began work in April.* It probably makes no sense to an observer from a contractual society that a person could be effectively barred from the lifelong employment system itself by asking for a contract guaranteeing such employment. Clearly, it is illogical. But then, so much in Japan seems illogical. Indeed, the whole society sometimes seems to be inscrutable.

Most inscrutable of all is the way the media criticize the

---

*Japanese companies generally make formal decisions on the employment of prospective college or high school graduates in November or shortly thereafter, but new employees are not initiated until April of the following year.

social system, the way they track down the "real culprit" responsible for any sort of problem. Some incident will trigger heated discussion and wide coverage by the media. In trying to identify the ultimate source of the problem, they escalate their logic, connecting one thing with another, until they find that the culprit is the system itself.

This escalation was seen lately when a few child suicides occurred in rapid succession. Child suicides are nothing new. Their number has not suddenly risen, nor do they seem especially typical of postwar Japanese society. Furthermore, the rate in Japan is not particularly high by international standards. Nevertheless, the media were quick to attribute the phenomenon first to the overemphasis on scholastic achievement in school, then to the university entrance exams, and finally to the system of education itself. Once something is declared guilty, people assume that the problem can be solved merely by eliminating or rectifying the culprit.

Behind the phenomenon of what we call "examination hell" is the desire on the part of students to attend a first-rate university, which gives them the credentials to apply for employment in a first-rate company. The Japanese university differs fundamentally from its counterparts elsewhere. There is a grading system, but basically one need merely attend for four years to graduate. The same is true of companies; once someone manages to enter a good company, assuming he does not commit a serious crime or offense, he need not worry about losing his job. He is assured a livelihood at the same time that he is assured a good chance for promotion. The system is a sort of gamble with no risk, a redeemable lottery ticket. Even if there is no guarantee that everyone will find first-rate jobs, people are convinced that the investment in an education will pay off. As long as there is some truth to this belief in the redeemable lottery ticket, people will rush to buy them. And it is only natural that some will be trampled to death in the race. Newspapers are fond of criticizing this notion, but that is sheer hypocrisy. To write for a newspaper, one must first have graduated from a top university. To criticize the stampede, one must have run with the herd!

What characterizes Japanese society is a kind of seniority system. According to that principle, one's accumulated achievements in school and on the job are measured by the number of years of enrollment or service, which, in turn, is converted into rank or status. Of course, one's ability or competence is taken into consideration in evaluating one's achievements, but, in either case, rank is conferred on the basis of seniority.

Seniority System—A Prototype

The seniority system is not limited to larger companies; it exists in small companies as well. That may surprise many, for it is often assumed that smaller companies are different, but if we look closely, it becomes apparent that the only big difference between large and small companies is in the means by which workers' achievement is converted to rank. To illustrate my point, let me briefly describe the postwar careers of some printing, binding, and box-making company owners with whom I have worked for nearly thirty years.

Mr. Harada is now in his mid-sixties and retired. By nature he is a devoted craftsman. He is generally taciturn and even morose, so much so that people tend to give him a wide berth until they get to know him. Then they discover how warm and dependable he is. When he has had a few drinks, he waxes eloquent and holds forth at an amazing pace on his career and experiences. Interested in hearing about his life, I made a point of going drinking with him until late at night on several occasions.

His family were poor farmers in a prefecture near Tokyo. Before finishing grade school, he was sent to the port city of Chōshi as an umbrella maker's apprentice so that the family would have one less mouth to feed. As an apprentice, he was provided with the essentials, but he was obliged to work every day of the year for no pay and to suffer abuse from the owner as well. Though not one to give up easily, eventually he could stand the man's cruelty no longer, and he ran off. Like most runaways, he had nowhere to go. Thinking Tokyo his best bet, the penniless boy started the long walk to the capital, sleeping outdoors with almost nothing to eat. Because he had never before set foot in Tokyo, he wandered aimlessly for a while. Finally, when he was about to collapse from hunger and fatigue he happened to catch sight of a scrap of paper pasted on a wall, advertising a job for an apprentice. Desperate, he answered the ad, which was from a bindery. As it turned out, that determined his career.

The bindery, at the time one of the largest in Japan, was housed in a three-story wooden building that had been built after the 1923 earthquake. Apprentices lived on the third floor, while the owner and his family occupied a portion of the second. Hours were from 8 a.m. to 8 p.m. daily, with night and late night work for half of each month. The shop was closed only two days a month, on the first and the fifteenth. It followed this schedule until the mid-1950s, as did most small shops and firms.

Naturally apprentices were expected to clean in the mornings and to tidy up after the day's work. Harada recalls, "I'm small now, but I was even smaller then. 'Long about seven each morning while I was out front sweeping with a broom taller than I was, the university students with their briefcases and square caps would pass on their way to school. I couldn't even imagine the sort of life they led, but how I envied them!" But when he had learned something about the workings of the factory, he concluded that his prospects for the future were not so dim after all.

The seniority system in stores that he described sounded like something from the early eighteenth century. As in the Tokugawa period (1603–1867), prewar Japanese wholesalers and large retail stores had a precise system of ranks. The four lowest ranks—*detchi, tedai, bantō, ōbantō*—were roughly equivalent to today's general employee, supervisor, section chief, and department manager. The next higher rank, *yadoiri*, did not have to live in, and the highest, *norenwake*, was allowed to set up a subsidiary. The seniority system differed somewhat in small factories such as Harada's, where the ranks were apprentice (*kozō*), journeyman (*shokunin*), and foreman (*shokuchō*).

Stores set up *norenwake* as heads of their own chain stores, where they sold the parent store's merchandise. Generally, these subsidiary heads eventually paid the main store back and gained their independence. In factories the system was much the same. Foremen would start a subsidiary factory, subcontracting for the parent factory. They were free to cultivate their own clientele, provided they did not take business away from the main factory. In this way they eventually became independent.

Allowing independence for senior workers had profound economic implications for the system. When parent stores and factories were growing rapidly, especially in times of prosperity, it was relatively easy to achieve independence, but it was much harder in times of depression. As a rule, one's salary rose with promotions through the ranks of foreman and *ōbantō*. When senior workers were unable to achieve independence, the ranks above did not open up to allow people below to rise. If nothing was done, the entire organization aged. At the same time, some workers had to be allowed the privilege of moving out of the dormitory, which meant providing housing, and wages could not be totally frozen. The only way to recover these costs was to raise the price of products, which would decrease their competitiveness. To avoid that situation, it was imperative for the entire business to keep the circulation of personnel going by setting up a certain number of workers as subsidiaries and taking on apprentices, who worked for virtually nothing.

Apprentices, for their part, received no salary at first, but they were provided with the essentials, and they knew that if they worked hard and learned the trade they would eventually become their own boss. With enough effort, they might eventually become as prosperous as their employers. This motivated them not just to work hard but to learn the trade as well. It also increased their loyalty to the company.

Some journeymen struck out on their own. Because one could earn more as an independent journeyman, some preferred this route as a means of leading a comfortable, more relaxed life. Generally, income came from a form of contracting. Typesetters, in particular, often chose this arrangement, agreeing to do a page for a certain fee. In this case, they subcontracted only their expertise. But while their income was higher, their future prospects were limited. Of the company heads I knew, none had been independent journeymen; every one had worked for one company until he established his own company. I will explain the reason for this later.

Such was the seniority system in small-to-medium-sized

businesses. There might be a parent company, primary subsidiaries, secondary subsidiaries, and independent journeymen, all tied together in a communal system. The principle of seniority governed not only the hierarchy of employees but the entire web of relationships within the company group. Even after Harada achieved complete independence, if asked to do work for his former employer he would always give it first priority, no matter what the inconvenience. Most of his career had been spent this way. What is interesting historically is that this system of seniority developed in the Tokugawa period, not after the introduction of Western capitalism in the Meiji era (1868–1912). For this reason, it is part and parcel of the traditional social structure.

Spiritual Satisfaction

Today it is hard to imagine how intensely subsidiary owners worked when they first gained independence. Literally, they did the work of president, journeymen, and apprentices themselves. Still, work for the parent company was irregular. Sometimes work went on day and night and fell behind even then; at other times there would be no work at all. Naturally, when there was no work there was no income. I had the following conversation with Tashiro, head of his own boxmaking company.

"I'm rather proud to say that I was successful. The difference between success and failure was in the way you either used or wasted your slack time."

"What did you do?"

"Someone once told me to go around town and pass out business cards. He said take a hundred cards and spend the whole day at it. It's easy enough to say but, heck, I'm a craftsman, and craftsmen just don't do that kind of thing. Also, you don't like doing something with no guarantee of a profit. So when there was no work, you were always tempted to do piecework for another company and get cash on the spot. But that's degrading yourself; you become just another independent journeyman. Once you did that, you were as good as finished as a businessman."

So he decided to go out and hunt for customers, and, in the process, he got a feel for doing business.

"If you pass out a thousand cards you're sure to get one or two takers, and if you do your work well they'll be your clients for life. It's a good investment."

This is the sort of person responsible for Japan's postwar recovery. Though their businesses were reduced to ashes and they were penniless, they did not give up. They were capable of running a business singlehandedly. In Harada's words, "I don't know anything about anything else. But when it comes to binding I can hold my own against anyone. Just give me a little leather, a brush, and some paste." Tashiro said the same sort of thing. Harada's four-story building is now filled with the latest equipment. But were he to lose it all, he could still manage nicely. After all, a machine merely does the work of hands more efficiently. Thus, even in a shack amid the postwar ruins he was able to carry on. By that time he was no longer dependent on his parent company. It gave him a certain amount of work, but because he was thoroughly familiar with doing business himself, he was able to build his own clientele. With some leather, a brush, and paste, he built his business into a large factory in less than thirty years. This can hardly be called a miracle. The system, plus his own efforts, made it all possible.

The majority of Japan's businesses have followed this pattern, working in a system that dates back to the Tokugawa (Edo) period. The system may appear to have changed somewhat, but the structure is basically the same, as is the underlying spirit. When I complimented Harada on his factory and his machines, he answered, "Heck, when I was an apprentice things were much more impressive than this." I assumed at the time that he was being modest. But because the machines then in use were primitive, to say the least, clearly what he meant was that it is not fancy buildings or machines that make a factory what it is. It is the spirit—an almost sacred attitude toward one's place of work.

According to Harada, the wooden floor of the old factory had been polished like a training hall for the martial arts, and everyone, including the owner, removed his footwear upon entering, even in the dead of winter. At the entrance was a small Shinto altar. No smoking was allowed during working hours, and no one engaged in idle chatter. At New Year, they made an offering to the paper cutter and hung a sacred Shinto rope on it. In some ways, he said, it resembled a monastery more than a factory.

"But those were the good old days. Today . . ."

"Yes, but in your factory you still hang a rope on the paper cutter and make offerings, don't you?" I asked.

"We will as long as I'm alive, anyway. That's the only attitude to have toward work."

As he said this, he cast a wistful glance at his new machines. Work, in his mind, equaled asceticism. It is not purely an economic pursuit, but a search for spiritual satisfaction.

This sort of spirit was the basis of order within companies. There was no need for company rules and regulations. Everyone responded to this communal spirit instead of to formal rules characteristic of modern functional groups. Harada had participated as a boy in this sort of spiritual community, and he remembered that time with nostalgia. The same held true with a family of companies, which was itself a close-knit group. This is one reason that journeymen who struck out on their own could not become heads of companies. Though they were extremely skilled, they were not really an integral part of the community. Although they might achieve the seniority of accomplishment and high wages for their piecework, they could not be conferred a rank within the community commensurate with their technical competence.

The Sacred and the Profane

I once conducted a survey for the Japan National Broadcasting Corporation (NHK) on corporate deities and found that it is not at all uncommon for a company to have a Shinto altar. In many, the entire staff, including the president, visit an Inari shrine once a month. They all have identical box lunches which they eat together as if partaking of communion. One of Japan's largest companies, known for having the most modern management system, has its own shrines. One of the top executives is a Shinto priest. Every year he travels around the country to well over a hundred of the company's branch offices and factories where he officiates at ceremonies held in their branch shrines. This mammoth corporation, with yearly sales of more than 1.5 trillion yen, is at once a marvelously efficient functional group and a spiritually close-knit communal organization.

But while corporate deities may help explain the communalism of Japanese companies, they cannot explain their functional efficiency as well. In fact, management is thoroughly rational and modern. It certainly does not rely on divine inspiration. In a sense, all Japanese companies have a dual structure; they are at once a functional and a communal group. A functional group does not work unless it is also communal by virtue of being able to translate functional achievements into a rank or status in the communal hierarchy.

The spirit of Japanese capitalism perhaps cannot be understood apart from this dualism. The unseen principles that permeate the social structure and govern the mentality and behavior of individual Japanese must also be placed in this context. In this book, I will try to explain exactly what those principles are and how the spirit of our capitalism evolved.

2

CONSANGUINEOUS AND TERRITORIAL SOCIETIES

The social structure of a nation and the value system of its people are products of a long, gradual process of evolution that is guided by innumerable factors. Every society differs in numerous, sometimes subtle, ways, but they can be roughly classified into two types, consanguineous and territorial.

Pseudo-consanguineous Society

Many people believe that Japan is a consanguineous society. This is a misconception. The political scientist Komuro Naoki and I once discussed this point on a nationally broadcast TV program, and Komuro startled many viewers with the following statement:

> There is one vitally important sociological concept that applies to every country but Japan. It is the concept of religion and norms based on contracts. Americans and Europeans have no trouble understanding Chinese or Koreans, because theirs are all contractual societies. But when it comes to the ways of thinking in the noncontractual society of Japan, they are at a loss; Japanese seem impossible to understand.

Nor is our social system based on blood relations. On the surface we appear to be a consanguineous society, but we are not. Adopting a male heir into a family, for example, is an ancient custom in Japan, but in a genuine consanguineous society it would be unthinkable. The Japanese family system is an ideology more than an institution tied together by blood. Think of the father in the Japanese family: Once a tyrant, since the Second World War he has held less power than his wife and children. In Germany, which is a true consanguineous society, the father is still the undisputed authority in the family.

Komuro speaks of both contracts and blood relations, but I will focus here only on blood relations and take up contracts in the next chapter.

Japan should be called a pseudo-consanguineous society. Granted our fictitious kinship system functions in much the same way as a genuine kinship system, but it is not the real thing. It is an ideology.

The principles of consanguinity in Japan have been codified only in the old Imperial House Act of 1890. According to the act, revised after World War II, only male descendants of the emperor may ascend the throne, and the order of ascension is determined by order of birth. No exceptions are permitted. Males cannot be adopted into the imperial family. In a true consanguineous society, the principle of nonadoption permeates society as a whole and shapes its history, as among Arabs and in overseas Chinese merchant communities. In Japan, it is limited to the imperial family.

Illustrations of the nonconsanguineous principle abound in Japanese history. Toyotomi Hideyoshi (1536–98), the military ruler who reunified the country in the later sixteenth century, was adopted into the aristocratic family of Konoe Ryūzan and succeeded to the position of chief adviser to the emperor. The son of a peasant, Hideyoshi had no blood ties whatsoever with the illustrious descendants of the Fujiwara. Uesugi Yōzan (1751–1822), the enlightened daimyo of Yonezawa, whom I will take up in chapter 7, was adopted by the Uesugi family from another daimyo family. The Kamakura shogunate (1185–1333) was established by Minamoto no Yoritomo (1147–99), but it was not a consanguineous group of Minamoto clan kinsmen. The Taira clan, as it is portrayed in the medieval narrative masterpiece *The Tale of the Heike,* appears to have been more like a consanguineous group and is generally thought to have been so; but if one looks closely at the *Heike,* one can find nonconsanguineous elements, and, in any case, the work is not historically accurate.

The Third Race

Yoritomo set up his shogunate on a territorial base, in the Kantō area, instead of building it on one blood-related clan. For this reason, he chose to remain in Kamakura, the geopolitical center of the region, instead of administering the country from its capital, Kyoto, as did the Taira clan. But Japan did not become a territorial society. If it had, the emperor system would have been rendered obsolete. For in a true territorial society, groups form solely on the basis of territory without reference to blood lineage.

In Rome, during the first century of the Christian era, we see the formation of a true territorial group: the Christians. As their numbers grew, some began to call this first generation of Christians the "third race," an appellation originally implying higher spirituality than Jews or Gentiles. The Romans likened the spread of Christianity to an epidemic; as soon as a church was established the strange "affliction" reached out, affecting the thinking of Greeks,

Romans, Asians, and Africans alike. This new "third race" unified people of many languages, races, and cultures into the body of the church. Its members formed a community of spiritual brothers and sisters who shared a territory.

While Christianity in Rome grew through such communities, religious traditions in Judea, the birthplace of Christianity, did not accept racial or cultural heterogeneity. The Jews, a Semitic people, have strictly preserved a consanguineous system. Even though Christianity grew up in their synagogues, the Jews did not form a territorially based group, and because of this they were eventually separated from the Christian church.

The territorial principle is reflected in the New Testament. The lineage of Jesus is described in the Gospel According to St. Matthew, but in the Epistle to the Hebrews, which is in fact addressed to the Jews, his lineage is disavowed when Christ is described as a "high priest after the order of Melchizedek." Melchizedek, who "was without father or mother or genealogy," appears in the Old Testament, where he blesses Abraham and receives a tenth of his wealth. Interestingly enough, their chance encounter came about by a territorial relationship rather than blood ties.

In a territorial society, all those who perform some function within the communal group are granted membership, in this case in the church, and are afforded rights. In the community created by the third race, there were no rights based on blood lineage. For this reason Christ was regarded as lacking a genealogy. Even if his genealogy had been acknowledged, it would have meant nothing. The principle was developed by the Christians, who finally also obliterated distinctions of nationality and even class. But to the Romans, the idea of an aristocrat sitting next to a slave in church, or being blessed by a priest who was a former slave, was scandalous. Hence the persecution of the Christians.

The United States offers a contemporary example of a nearly territorial society. Be one royalty or commoner, regardless of national origin, as long as a person lives in the United States he or she is considered a member of the American "third race." Even the child of alien parents becomes an American if he or she is born on American soil, with the attendant advantages and disadvantages. It used to be that male children would eventually be subject to the draft. I know several Japanese nationals who were astonished to receive draft notices from the U.S. government. To members of a territorial society, however, there is nothing unnatural in associating citizenship, its rights and duties, with place of birth.

The Company Community

The Meiji government was stimulated, and sometimes plagued, by rivalry among clan cliques. The same was true of the Freedom and People's Rights movement, which was led by anti-oligarchy clan cliques. These cliques make an interesting study, for they do not lend themselves to classification as either consanguineous or territorial. They were centered on feudal domains, but clans were not territorial groups. A territorial group depends on its geographical base; without that it ceases to function, or simply goes out of existence. The Japanese clans, however, like the society of the Jews, were not fatally splintered when deprived of their land. They survived in the form of cliques, but unlike the Jewish community, these cliques were no more consanguineous in the Meiji period than are their present-day descendants, intraparty factions. As powerful as was his hold on the Chōshū clique, the Meiji statesman Yamagata Aritomo (1838–1922) could not pass its leadership on to his son.

The clan cliques were, in fact, functional groups with a close-knit, pseudo-consanguineous communal structure. As long as they had a function, they existed. When they lost their function, they ceased to exist; when they recovered their function, they revived. Because they were an inherent part of the social structure, they were not affected by such formal developments as the 1880 Constitution or the establishment of a parliamentary system.

It is the same in a company, which is both a functional group and a community. It needs a function to exist and must be communal to function. Indeed, new members are initiated into the company community in the same way that a whole territorial group becomes a third race. The company screening examinations, followed by a series of induction ceremonies, are all rites of passage. Then the new employee undergoes a period of training. Only when this is completed is he given duties in the functional organization. Once admitted to the company community, one naturally stays for the rest of one's career. And because acceptance into the company community is an extracontractual arrangement, there is no such thing as a lifelong employment contract.

Despite the lack of a contract, workers in the lifelong employment system do not fear dismissal, since dismissal is regarded as an unfair labor practice. But workers do lose their jobs. Their job security hinges on whether or not they are full-fledged members of the communal group. Among workers doing the same job in the same company there are regular employees—members of the company community—and full- or part-time temporary workers, who are not members of the group. Those in the latter group can be dismissed at any time.

The distinction between the two categories of employees within a company is as sharp as that between members and nonmembers of a consanguineous society. The life-long employment and seniority systems apply only to those in the company community, not to anyone outside the group. The moment one is admitted as a regular member of the company one acquires certain basic rights, just as a child does when it is born into a consanguineous society and is accepted, not on the basis of lineage, but of place of birth. Dismissing a regular employee amounts to separating him from his kith and kin—a sort of disinheritance—something that no society takes lightly. For those who have not been initiated into the company community, however, even tenure means nothing. No matter how many years temporary workers work for a company, they never acquire rights. They can be dismissed at any time and no one will question the propriety of the action.

The system is not without its critics. Labor unions call for eliminating discrimination against temporary workers and conferring community membership on all employees. No one, however, calls for the dissolution of the company community.

One can find examples of companies that have integrated all their employees into the communal group, as well as companies that were integrated from the start. Even so, these companies inevitably employ subcontractors, which are small communities in themselves, affiliated with but not belonging to the contracting company. Subcontractors work together with the company but still remain outside the company community. The main company-subcontractor relationship resembles that of regular and provisional employees. Only business dealings tie the groups together. Once the business relationship is terminated, the subcontractor community automatically ceases to exist as far as the main company is concerned. The effect is similar to dismissing a temporary employee, except that in the former case the parent company may be responsible for the dissolution of the subcontractor community, not the dismissal of its individual workers.

Why are certain people excluded from the company community? The answer is that in times of recession or when the company is not doing well, they can be laid off without damaging anyone's reputation. Whether a provisional worker quits or is fired, all that happens is that his role in the functional organization ceases. It is not unfair because he is not being ostracized from the community, and neither his reputation nor that of the company suffers. On the other hand, dismissing a full-fledged employee— driving him from the company community—is unfair, for it will hurt the person's pride and his reputation, not only within the immediate community but in the trade and business world as well.

As noted earlier, regular members of a company will sometimes commit crimes or blunders of such serious proportions that they must be let go. Even so, they are usually not dismissed. Instead, they are allowed to tender their resignation and thus "voluntarily" exit from the communal group.

Group Honor

A regular employee may be fairly dismissed when his behavior is judged to have tarnished the company's honor. Then the worker is expelled primarily from the company community and only incidentally from the functional organization. It is therefore possible for the company's functionally most competent member to be dismissed.

The Japanese concept of honor is essentially foreign to countries with strong traditions of individualism. There, people speak of the individual's honor, but not so much of family honor or responsibility toward clan or community. The latter expressions sound hopelessly old-fashioned to members of those societies.

To illustrate the concept of group honor, let us look at the case of an individual arrested for deviant sexual behavior. In many instances, the person cannot be punished by law. If he is a drifter, for example, someone with no connection with a communal group, he has no great problem, even if his behavior is publicized. But when he is a full-fledged member of a company, especially one that is well known, it is an entirely different situation. It can be argued that such personal behavior has nothing to do with the company as a functional unit and has no overt effect on that function, but it profoundly affects the honor of the company community. This is sufficient ground for dismissal. It would be futile to claim unfair dismissal in such a case. Protest would only further damage the personal reputation of the offender.

The concept of collective honor is unknown in American companies. During the Lockheed bribery scandal, a Japanese reporter visited the head offices of the Lockheed Corporation and later reported his amazement at the American employees' total lack of embarrassment over the scandal. In Japan, if employees of a company involved in a scandal were to be so nonchalant or personally detached, they would be subjected to even fiercer public condemnation. What the reporter did not realize is that the American attitude is natural in a contractual society. The workers at Lockheed, as in any American company, contracted to work for the functional organization in exchange for wages. Because there is no company community, there is no sense of personal responsibility for the group's behavior. Indeed, they had no reason whatsoever to feel embarrassed about the wrongs their company committed, especially before the Japanese reporter.

Japanese reporters take it for granted that members of a company community will feel ashamed when their management is involved in a scandal. One reason is that the company's honor has been compromised. Second, they assume that when a company has wronged society as a whole, its employees will naturally feel humiliated vis-à-vis the public.

Japanese newspapers are often critical of the peculiarly Japanese concept of honor, but an examination of newspaper style shows that, in fact, they themselves subscribe to it wholeheartedly. They commonly refer, for example, to a criminal's "defiant" attitude. During the Grumman scandal, it was the "insolent" attitude of Nisshō-Iwai executives they found offensive. To a reporter's mind, these people should have been apologetic. Perhaps unconsciously, reporters consider themselves representatives of the public; hence they assume that all criminal suspects should demonstrate humiliation toward the press corps.

The World's Safest City

The concept of group honor and the feeling of humiliation society expects from a wrongdoer have enormous social implications. Among these implications are both advantages and disadvantages. Surely, one of the greatest benefits is that society's expectations function as an effective crime deterrent. Professor Miyazawa Kōichi, criminologist at Tokyo's Keiō University, once recounted an observation made by a proprietor of a shop near the university soon after the newspapers reported admission irregularities there. In the proprietor's words, the entire faculty of Keiō seemed to slink about, hunched over with eyes cast down. It is the same phenomenon. A university is at once a functional and a communal group. When the organization suffers dishonor, its entire membership loses face, as a group and as individuals.

There are obvious demerits to this particular social function. One is that an organization will do everything it can to conceal crimes committed by its members. Another is that just to be accused of a crime is enough to cause one's organization to lose face, and it may result in dismissal.

Crime is one of the many problems faced today by modern societies whose traditional communal bodies have collapsed. Because the pace of industrialization, urbanization, depopulation of rural areas, and destruction of the rural community has been faster in Japan than in any other country, it would not be surprising if we had a serious crime problem. Tokyo, which was transformed from an almost deserted wasteland after the war to a pulsing megalopolis of more than eleven million people virtually overnight, should be the world's most crime-ridden city. Instead, there, as elsewhere in Japan, the crime rate, especially for serious crimes, has been steadily declining. It is not possible to construct a consanguineous society artificially, nor can a territorial society become communal in the absence of a unifying ideology. Fortunately for Japan, an equivalent unifying effect has been achieved by the evolution of a pseudo-consanguineous society, and this has had untold influence on the crime rate and deviant behavior.

Needless to say, communal groups can also be found in parts of the United States. A good example is Salt Lake City. Founded by Mormons, it is a safe, clean, friendly city with a communal spirit. Communal groups exist even in New York City. I know of a dormitory belonging to a new Christian sect located in a particularly dangerous section of the city, where no one would dream of going out after dark. The dormitory's doors are never locked at night, and one might leave a suitcase unattended in the lobby for days without fear of losing it. Members represent all races and educational and work backgrounds. Some have money and some do not. The membership includes ex-convicts, as well as former drug addicts. All are bound together by religion, without regard to blood relations. When one enters their dormitory, one begins to understand what a territorially based "third race" is all about. At the same time, one can understand what made possible the tragedy at Jonestown, Guyana, where over nine hundred members of a religious cult committed mass suicide. Compared with the extremes in the ideology and practical circumstances of Jonestown, the Japanese group demands are far easier to live with.

Functional Irrationality

Because a group in Japan must be communal if it is to function, an individual who wants to work within a group must first be granted membership; one cannot belong to one communal group and function effectively in another. An employee is a member of a team, and must always put the interests of the group ahead of personal interests. If he tries to function independently, his superiors are apt to remark, "He's a competent guy, but he doesn't know how to cooperate," or "He's capable all right, but he doesn't understand team play." In other words, one might be evaluated highly as a member of the functional group yet rated low as a member of the communal group. Double standards of evaluation are only natural when rank is determined by seniority; no matter how competent one might be, one is expected to know one's place. Indeed, this is inevitable when a group can function only as a community. Understandably, companies are eager to employ people who have participated in team sports in their youth.

The dual structure of the Japanese company has profound implications for its functional rationality. A functional group exists to attain some goal. In the case of an army, the goal is to win; it does not exist to lost battles, and will cease to exist if it loses too many men. An enterprise exists to make a profit. If it does not, it eventually goes bankrupt and likewise ceases to exist. It does not exist to lose money. At times, however, both armies and companies deliberately accept losses. In view of their function, common sense tells us that they do so only as a tactic to which they resort with the expectation of future gains. Japanese companies that export at a loss have good reason for doing so, but then they are accused of dumping.

If they were exclusively functional groups, such charges would be justified. But as we have seen, Japanese companies are communal groups as well. Communal groups differ from functional ones in that for them existence is a goal in itself. For this reason, a Japanese company will operate at a loss if it must to keep its communal structure intact, that is, to preserve jobs. Needless to say, members make sacrifices for the sake of the group, forgoing raises and, at times, taking wage cuts. This they willingly do, for they clearly perceive that the very survival of their community is at stake.

Village Community

The phenomenon of individual sacrifices for the sake of a communal group is not confined to Japan. It can be observed in the West as well. There, too, people derive certain satisfaction in sacrifices, and therein discover a reason for living. In addition, they render much service to strengthen blood and territorial relationships. But the communal group they belong to is most often the very community in which they live, not a company. The company remains merely a functional group, separate from the communal habitat. One might say Westerners commute between the two groups.

In *Hanshinpo e no tabi* (Journey away from progress) Nishibe Susumu offers a portrait of one such community in Britain: Folkestone, a small village about eight miles from Cambridge.

> If asked to describe my nine-month stay in Folkestone in a word, I would say it has been most delightful. Though located in the midst of an ailing nation, it is such a relaxing place that one living here might conclude that the British disease is a form of euphoria. Above all, one feels a sense of community. Clearly, the villagers work hard to preserve it. Yet they are so casual in their efforts that one could easily overlook them, and assume that the harmony here was a natural phenomenon. . . .
>
> As for the notorious snobbishness of the British gentleman, I've yet to encounter it. What snobbishness there is seems to have been tempered by just the right amount of exposure to modern civilization and working class attitudes. The fact that nearly everyone but me owns an automobile indicates, I think, that the village has not turned its back on modernization. The villagers

are quite interested in following modern trends and realize the advantages. But, at the same time, they exhibit that conservatism that is the forte of the British. To them London is the evil city, and while they realize that they must modernize, they are determined to do so carefully and at their own pace. . . .

I've developed a habit of taking words like reform, progress, development, and change with a grain of salt. Perhaps the reason life in this village is so serene is that the people here think the same way. In the morning after a breakfast of bacon, eggs, toast, and tea with milk the men leave for work in neighboring towns, and the women busy themselves with house-cleaning and tea parties. Boys play soccer around the clock and girls are constantly breaking up with one group of friends only to join another. On Sunday, the older girls go horseback riding while the adults putter in their gardens. For their vacation, the whole family motors to Spain for sunbathing.

While villagers in Britain leave their communities each morning and commute to work, the reverse is the case in Japan. Here one is always a part of the company community, and the neighborhood is merely the place one happens to sleep. In both cases, temporarily leaving the communal group does not mean severing relations. In both cases, one is glad to work for the good of the communal group but resents being asked to sacrifice for something outside it. Japanese will gladly work overtime for nothing, yet they are loath to do anything for their neighborhood.

Surely, the epitome of communal company life is found in the large corporations such as Sony that employ many young women in their factories. The factories are literally communities in themselves. The girls sleep together in company dormitories and, after hours, can attend lessons in tea ceremony, flower arranging, cooking, etiquette, and general education, all offered at company expense. What was once a system of cruel exploitation has become a means of self-fulfillment.

The present-day system does not differ fundamentally from that of Harada's factory, as described in the last chapter. Just as factory girls do today, he slept in company lodgings as night, and during the day had the skills and manners of a craftsman drummed into his head. In those days, too, management assumed the responsibility to contribute to employees' personal development. Although this did not involve an outlay of funds as today, management did not interfere when workers pursued education. Many apprentices attended night schools. Especially popular were correspondence courses, such as *Waseda kōgiroku* (Waseda lecture series). They accounted for a good percentage of all publishing in those days.

Like the seniority system, this kind of communal management developed in the Tokugawa period, not in modern times. Rapid modernization enlarged its scale, especially after the Second World War, but the system basically has not changed. Japan's economic development rests on the Tokugawa heritage, which I will discuss further in later chapters.

The communal structure of Japanese companies made it possible for the economy to cope relatively easily with the first oil crisis and the recession that followed. The price a company can receive for a product is, of course, largely dictated by the market, so companies had no choice but to minimize losses by rationalizing, especially in conserving energy. Streamlining demands great efforts on the part of employees. Because Japanese employees take a personal interest in the welfare of their company, they cooperated eagerly.

But as we have seen, the same determination to preserve the group can lead it to function as a loss, if that is necessary for its survival. Carried to extremes, the company's original, practical function becomes a means to a different end—the preservation of the communal group. This does not usually create serious problems when a company is privately owned, as there is a limit to the losses it can absorb without going bankrupt. But when a company has virtually unlimited access to funds, as monopolistic or government-run enterprises and national and local governing bodies do, the burden on society can be heavy. The classic example is the Japan National Railways— sometimes called the JNR Family—perennially able to pass its staggering losses on to the government and ultimately the taxpayers.*

No doubt it is an intuitive perception of the danger of a spreading Japanese disease that explains the Japanese people's reluctance to heed reformist calls for the nationalization of industry. The reformist parties' protests against LDP ties to monopolistic capitalists and their appeals to give priority to citizen welfare over that of capitalists are attractive. But what reformers fail to see is that the demands of the communal group supersede logic. And what makes the demands of the communal group of absolute importance is the absoluteness of consensus.

The Power of Consensus

The absolute power of consensus in Japan is a problem of immense proportions. On the simplest level, it can be seen in the problem of high school girls who engage in prostitution. When counseled by authorities, they usually say something like, "It's enjoyable for the man and for me, too. We're not hurting anybody, and I'm able to make

---

*The Japan National Railways have since been privatized, divided into several regional railroads, which on the whole do well.

money. What's wrong with it?" One is hard put to counter such an argument. Because both parties consented, they consider their behavior permissible. Consensus supersedes any legal or ethical constraints; no one, these girls believe, has the right to interfere once the consensus is achieved.

The most powerful prewar communal group was undoubtedly the army, which put its own interests above those of the nation, ultimately leading Japan into the disastrous Second World War. Indeed, the consensus of the Council of Three Army Chiefs—chief of general staff, minister of war, and inspector-general of military education—who represented the army, was similarly extralegal and carried more weight than the will of the emperor. Under the prewar Constitution of the Greater Japanese Empire, the emperor was legally responsible for the appointment and dismissal of the prime minister; in reality, the council controlled the process. After the emperor appointed a prime minister, the council customarily selected a new minister of war. When they were unhappy with the emperor's decision, they simply refused to select a new minister and, unable to form a cabinet, the new prime minister had no choice but to resign. The best postwar example of a communal organization gone wild is the General Council of Trade Unions of Japan, which engineers strikes to preserve its own existence.

People tend to single out such groups for criticism and fail to realize that they operate under the same principles as other groups in Japan. Each reflects the social structure and the value system of the Japanese, and, in each case, members are sincere in their efforts to promote their group. When we understand this, we will be in a better position to reconsider why our country has been dubbed Japan Inc., and why the Japanese people are called economic animals.

3

CONTRACT VERSUS CONSENSUS

In the last chapter, we discussed one misconception about Japanese society, the idea that it is consanguineous. Another common misconception is the belief that Japanese society lacks any basic conception of contract. In a discussion on this point, Komuro Naoki, the political scientist, commented incisively:

> It is simply not so. Japanese understand the concept of honoring a contract. The expression "A samurai never goes back on his word" is a good demonstration. In the world of Tokugawa merchants, too, one kept one's promises. Japan is, moreover, one of the few nations that has settled all of its foreign debts. Treaties are a kind of contract. How could a country that strictly abides by many kinds of contracts be said to lack a conception of contract?

To say that Japan is not a contractual society means that contracts do not critically influence the social structure; it does not mean that individuals lack faith or that they do not abide by decisions reached through group consensus. In Japan, the consensus system takes the place of contracts, which is why we are not identified as a contractual society. Because the distinction between contractual and consensual societies is not always clear, let us examine a classic example of a contractual society. Semitic society, especially that of the strongly traditional Islamic peoples, offers an illustrative case.

Islamic Contracts

In an article interpreting the Khomeini revolution in Iran, entitled "God Booted the Shah Out," U.D. Khan Yousufzai, a Moslem, discusses the Moslem conception of contracts. Let me quote from the article:

> To take the borrowing and lending of money as an example, let us say A borrows 100 yen from B and begins a business. If A's business shows a profit of 20 yen, then A pays B only 10 yen back. If he makes 300 yen, he pays B 150 yen. In other words, they share the profit equally. If, on the other hand, the business fails, A need not pay B back, with the understanding that should he later make a profit he will share it with B. This is the Islamic style of economics. It is based on a contract between man and God, closely resembling the concept of *tsukiai* (communal fellowship), which has existed in Japanese village communities since ancient times. Into this milieu, the Western concept of the contract—an agreement between two individuals—was introduced no more than a hundred years ago.

The similarity Yousufzai sees between contracts in the Islamic world and fellowship in Japanese villages is not altogether plausible, but the point is that the contract he is describing is one between God and man, not between individuals. Honoring a contract with another person is a natural consequence of honoring one's contract with God. And because both borrower and lender have made identical contracts with God, the terms of their agreement need not be discussed.

If we study the effect of religious ideas in history, we

find that the same was true in Western Europe. As Western society became more complex, so did the details of contracts, but ultimately both social systems can be traced back to the common heritage of Islam and Christianity, the Old Testament.

In the Islamic world, the content of the contract between the individual and God is of paramount importance. Second, there can be no contractual relationship between individuals who have not sealed identical contracts with God. Last but not least, because an atheist cannot conclude a contract, a Moslem cannot negotiate with him. The significance of this last point is frequently overlooked by Japanese visiting Islamic nations when they foolishly admit to being atheists.

While I was talking with Yousufzai, he sighed, "I simply cannot see why our system is so hard for you Japanese to understand." A Japanese is likely to interpret a Moslem's attitude as either discriminatory or derogatory. But because the two systems are so different, such misunderstandings are bound to occur.

The Japanese custom of swearing before heaven, earth, and the deities (*tenchi shinmei ni chikau*) is quite different from entering into a contract with God. When Japanese make such a pledge, they swear to each other to abide by their agreement and merely call on heaven, earth, and the deities to act as witnesses or guarantors. Parties reach a consensus and then swear to each other with a god as their witness that they will keep their word. Consensus precedes everything. The Bible forbids this. Christians and Moslems conclude a contract with God, promising Him they will keep their word, and while one party makes his pledge, the other listens. The two patterns are illustrated in Figure 1.

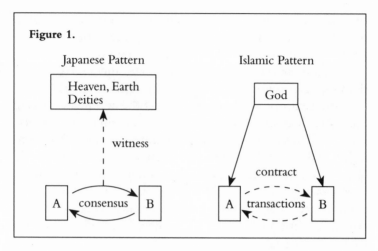

Figure 1.

Japanese Pattern   Islamic Pattern

Extralegality of Consensus

Both of the above systems have their own rationality and irrationality. As long as they operate within their own cultures they function smoothly. But when one of the systems is introduced into another culture, problems understandably arise that involve all aspects of the society. Such problems are now being encountered not only in Islamic nations but in Japan as well.

Japan's first experience of this sort came shortly after Christianity was introduced here in the sixteenth century. In a certain contemporary document is a concept that baffles Christians and Jews alike. Explaining it to Westerners is more difficult than explaining Islamic concepts of borrowing and lending and oaths based on a monotheistic religion to Japanese.

The document I speak of is called the *Nanban seishi* (The barbarian oath). There were at the time two oaths used by the authorities in their suppression of Christianity, one for non-Christians, by which they were made to swear they were not Christians, and another for Christians, by which they disavowed their religion. The latter was the *Nanban seishi*.

To lend credence to this oath, one needed a divine witness. But who? A Christian remained a Christian until the moment of his apostasy, and so he could not very well swear to heaven, earth, and deities in which he did not believe. The answer was simple. Christians were made to swear before the Christian god. Simply put, they swore to God that they did not believe in Him. Let me cite a passage.

> I do hereby solemnly swear on pain of the divine punishment of our heavenly Father, Mary, and the myriad angels: [If I break my vow] let me be handed over to the demons of Hell after my death, there to suffer eternal torment. And while still in this world let my body be wracked by disease, and let me be called leper.

As curiously contradictory as this document is, it makes perfect sense within the Japanese context, where consensus is absolute. The *Nanban seishi* was preceded by an agreement between the inquisitors and the Christian. Having reached a consensus, they merely needed someone to act as witness.

If one party to an agreement believes in Shinto and the other in Buddhism, Japanese will not hesitate to call on the gods and buddhas, respectively. If one of the parties happens to be a Christian, he of course should call on God as his witness. Consensus is more important than the gods, buddhas, or Christian god in Japan.

Unilateral Action

The implications of this consensus system extend far beyond the confines of religion to touch the course of the

nation itself. The Council of Three Army Chiefs, which I
mentioned in the previous chapter, is a case in point.

By law—by contract, as it were—the three army chiefs
reported directly to the emperor. Had Japan been a contractual society, their conferences could only have come
about as a result of the terms of their contracts with the
emperor. The relationship would have been like that of A
and B, as described by Yousufzai. Instead, after discussing
something among themselves and reaching a conclusion,
they called on the gods in the form of the "living deity,"
the emperor, to act as guarantor. To their minds, by
reaching a de facto decision without actually consulting
the emperor, they were not disregarding divine authority,
but rather demonstrating their faith in it. Nor did they
consider themselves disloyal subjects; on the contrary, they
believed themselves to be the most loyal Japanese in the
nation.

The imperial army is now defunct, but Japanese functional groups remain communal, and consensus means
more than law to them. But rather than calling on the
emperor to make their decisions final and absolute, people
now invoke the Constitution. In that the Constitution can
be used to support decisions that are really extralegal, the
situation recalls the *Nanban seishi*; it is like swearing, with
God as witness, that one does not believe in Him. The
same is true with many large Japanese corporations, as we
shall see.

It is easy enough to criticize this system, but pointless
really, because the same informal norms govern personal
behavior. In fact, were one to try running an organization
in Japan strictly according to contract, the same people
who criticize the present system would attack the new one
even more severely.

A Japanese Catholic priest once told me of the experiences of a French priest who came to Japan and was asked to assist in running a certain organization. He hired personnel strictly by contract, giving some three-year contracts and others five. Those who did not sign a contract had no job security and could be dismissed at any time. The contract was all that guaranteed their place within the organization. The priest assumed that those working without contracts understood this.

They did not. As far as they were concerned, their employment was based on mutual understanding and could not be terminated without establishing another understanding to that effect. Therefore, each time the priest had employees dismissed, they objected strongly. Although he explained that they had forfeited all rights when they agreed to work with no contract, in their minds he was guilty of the greatest of sins in a consensus society: unilateral action. He encountered similar problems when an employee's contract expired. In his thinking an employee's rights expired along with his contract. But in Japan one signs a contract with the understanding that when its term expires, employer and employee negotiate a new one.

What's in a Contract?

In Japan, a contract might be said to contain only one provision of overriding importance: that in the event of disagreement, both parties will discuss the matter in good faith. If a contract is concluded at all, it is no more than a document affirming the tradition of dialogue. To ignore a country's traditions, like the well-meaning but ignorant French priest, is to invite a host of problems.

Likewise, we Japanese must adapt ourselves to contractual society when we do business abroad. A manager I know set up operations in the United States, drawing up a Japanese-style employment contract. First he put in a clause requiring mutual good faith, but found that it had no effect whatsoever on his American employees. Next he deleted the clause altogether, but without any penalty provisions for breach of contract he was helpless to enforce it. When he consulted an American lawyer, the man only laughed. Indeed, according to Western custom, the manager was in the wrong, not the employees who took advantage of the loopholes in their contracts.

In Japan, too, people occasionally make use of loopholes. A well-publicized example is that of the Yomiuri Giants baseball team, who exploited a loophole in the rules covering the drafting of players in order to sign up the promising young pitcher Egawa Suguru in 1978. The "Egawa Problem" was in the news for nearly three months, during which time opprobrium was heaped on both Egawa and the Giants.* According to Western thinking, however, responsibility for the affair rests with those who drew up the rules. As far as I know, the dramatist and critic Yamazaki Masakazu, who has spent a great deal of time in the United States, is the only Japanese to make this point.

Humans everywhere are fallible creatures, and inevitably they will draw up imperfect contracts. In the West, when loopholes are discovered, an effort is usually made to close them. The Japanese manager of whom I spoke, after failing twice, finally succeeded in drawing up an airtight contract. This is because he was in America, a contractual

---

*The scandal spawned a neologistic verb "egawaru," meaning to act selfishly and underhandedly. When grade-school children were asked to name the three things they liked the least, they replied, in order, Egawa, green peppers, and the sumo Grand Champion Kitanoumi, whom many regarded as overconfident. [Trans.]

society, and had no choice. This is not the case in Japan. In spite of the Egawa scandal, to my knowledge no one suggested that the rules covering the drafting of players be revised. The loophole remains, but there is little chance that anyone else will exploit it, for while we have contracts in Japan, it is not the contract that has binding force. It is extralegal, supracontractual societal norms that keep Japanese in line. To defy these rules is to invite society's wrath.

The Revolving Door

Western contract-based organizations are, in fact, modeled on the Catholic church. I once gave a talk on the Society of Jesus before a group of Japanese businessmen. The Jesuit order was formed around Ignatius de Loyola in the fifteenth century, and its seven charter members signed an oath on Montmartre, on which they based the rules and organization of their group. When I said this, one of the men in the audience remarked that the group's start resembled the founding of a corporation. I laughed and replied that it was the other way around: Corporations are patterned after this group. Puritan society was formed the same way, based on the Mayflower Compact.

Whether a religious order, a nation-state, or a company, all Western organizations have but one base: a contract in the form of an oath, a constitution, or a set of articles of incorporation. By this contract a religious order sets forth its rules, a state enacts laws, and a company establishes regulations, all stipulating the individual's rights and obligations. A more specific work manual is then drawn up, spelling out job assignments and procedures. A contract is a prerequisite for admission into the functional group. Without a contract no work can be done, for there will be no way of knowing one's position in the organization, what its rules are, or what one's rights, obligations, responsibilities, or limitations are.

Western workers would not think of joining a corporation without first drawing up a contract. Grounded in the contract, organizations like chain stores, whose yearly employee turnover is 250 percent, can function. A Japanese company simply could not tolerate such a turnover. What makes the system work is the fact that the contract makes clear the terms of employment, and an employee need merely do what he has agreed to do. Naturally, he has no rights other than those granted in the contract, but then neither does he have any other obligations or responsibilities. The work for most employees in such organizations is simple in nature, and no matter how many years they put in, they do not rise; automatic promotion by seniority in such organizations is nonexistent. If a worker is chosen for a higher position, he receives a new contract describing his new duties along with his job limits, rights, obligations, and responsibilities.

Rules and Regulations

Whether superior or inferior to the Western system, the noncontractual Japanese employment system, like the seniority system discussed in chapter 1 has remained fundamentally the same from the Tokugawa period, through the Taishō era of small and medium industries, to the postwar era of large-scale industry. It is clearly not based on rules and regulations. Nevertheless, most Japanese companies have collections of company rules and regulations.

Komuro Naoki and I once visited a publisher that specializes in economics. During our conversation with the president, Komuro asked, half in jest, "Do you have company rules and regulations?" "Of course," was the president's prompt reply. "We published a volume called *Collection of Rules and Regulations.* So we have a fine set of bylaws for ourselves."

"Have you ever read it?"

"Are you kidding?" the president laughed.

Komuro looked around him. "Has anyone here read it?" he asked. Everyone in the room chuckled. "Then when you hire new personnel, how do you conclude a contract, and how do they learn what their obligations and responsibilities are?"

"When we hire someone, we just put them to work in the editorial or business office, and in four or five months they know how things are done."

"Then why do you need rules and regulations?"

"Well . . ."

Strange as it may seem, it is the same in all companies. From the president down, no one reads the company rules. When I asked the president of a securities firm about rules, he replied, "Certainly we have rules. We're authorized by the Ministry of Finance, you know. We have a formal set of rules and regulations." But when I asked if he had ever read them, he said no. More important, he said, was a set of five precepts that all employees recite every morning. It is less a collection of rules than a sort of family homily, embodying the basic moral principles of the communal group.

Rules do, however, have a very important function in Japanese organizations. They are used to preserve the traditional consensus system in much the same way as the gods are called on to guarantee the sincerity of the parties to an agreement.

I remember suggesting to a university professor one day

an innovation in the university system. He replied, "It sounds good, all right, but it would never work." When I asked him why, he answered, "If you were to suggest this, some official would come up with a provision that forbids it. After all, that's their job."

One might say, then, that organizations invoke laws and regulations when necessary to maintain the system. They are not, however, necessarily run according to the principles set forth in them.

In a discussion I had with the author Shiba Ryōtarō, he made the same point:

> Tōjō Hideki's authority derived from his superb knowledge of rules and by-laws, which he used like a shield. Whenever he opposed someone he would always come up with a provision that he could use against that person. In this way he was able to grasp more and more power. That's the scary thing about the system.

The rules Tōjō used were, of course, army regulations. Like company employees, military men do not read the regulations, so no one was in a position to challenge him. All one needed was to be told that his proposal went against regulations and he had no choice but to abandon it.

Naturally, General Tōjō invoked the rules only when it served his purposes. When it came to some of the most fundamental principles of the state, such as the relationship between the emperor and the three army chiefs, he could blithely ignore the law. Rules were used to protect the principle of consensus within the army. The same can be said of the bureaucracy today.

This principle functions not just for organizations but for society as a whole. We have, for example, a law covering foreign exchange. Like the Staple Food Control

Act, it is common knowledge that no one observes it. As long as one abides by social norms, one will not face censure even if one's action violates the letter of the law. But should social norms be violated, laws will be invoked.

Some time ago, the newspapers harshly criticized a former prime minister allegedly involved in a bribery scandal. But the legal charge against him was merely violation of the foreign exchange law. I seriously doubt that the newspapers are above such violations themselves, but still no one thought it odd that they should have inflated the case involving the prime minister. This is not surprising, because everyone knows that the newspapers' attitude toward the law is fundamentally the same as that of officials.

Needless to say, the same principle functions with regard to contracts. Contracts merely serve to support the traditional system of consensus. This is why parties to a contract pledge to act in good faith. According to experts, whether they expressly say so or not, all Japanese laws contain this element. If a contract goes against social norms, it is void. And if, like the French priest, one insists that such a contract is valid, one will encounter problems. Even so, if the person involved is a foreigner—that is, someone outside Japanese communal groups, alien to the psychology of the members of this society—Japanese are willing to compromise. But when it comes to a fellow Japanese, there is no leniency. A Japanese who attempts to impose rules on an organization will find himself expelled from it, or relegated to a harmless position, which is nearly the same as expulsion.

Parent-Child Contract

Put simply, a consanguineous group is not a contractual one; the parent-child relationship does not come about as the result of any contract. But a contract can produce a pseudo-parent-child relationship in a pseudo-consanguineous group. And because there are social norms covering the relations between parent and child, one need merely exchange a contract either on paper or verbally to the effect that a parent-child relationship exists. There is no need for setting down provisions in the contract. On this point, the Japanese "fellowship" resembles the Islamic contract. There, of course, religious law governs the individual's contract with God, so when A agrees to borrow money from B, there is no need for a detailed contract.

We often say that the Islamic world is a closed society or that it is inscrutable. To one unfamiliar with the unstated terms of contracts there, it will certainly seem incomprehensible. But as difficult as Islamic society might be for Japanese to comprehend, we can gain a certain amount of understanding through the Islamic law, *sharia*, the fundamental concepts of which are the same as those of Western law. What we Japanese do not realize is that Japan itself appears to outsiders even more closed and inscrutable.

While I was on my trip to the United States, I had an opportunity to talk with a State Department official in charge of Middle East affairs, and this topic came up. To sum up his words, problems concerning the Middle East are not easy to solve, but Americans believe they understand the countries involved. But while there is no major problem between Japan and the United States (at the time), Americans do not really understand Japan.

In Japan, contracting individuals say, in effect, "Let's make a promise." "O.K." That is all it takes to establish a pseudo-parent-child or fraternal relationship. The moral code that governs this fictive relationship is an unwritten law, knowledge of which is acquired only through experience; nowhere has it been codified. For this reason, no one other than a Japanese can enter into this relationship.

Indeed, individual Japanese are open, flexible, and polite. Moreover, we make efforts to see things from the other's point of view. But open, our society is not. It is therefore virtually impossible for Japan to import workers to meet even the most severe of labor shortages. Foreign laborers would want to enter a functional group based on a contract, but as long as they did not join a pseudo-consanguineous group, they could not.

To exaggerate a bit, one might say that to work in Japan, one is asked, "Please join our group," and one responds, "Thanks. Please watch out for me." There is nothing more, nor is anything more needed. It is a provisionless blood contract, as if the parties had agreed that from that day on employer and employee were parent and child.

But just what sort of psychology underlies this social structure? And how does the interaction of the two turn the communal group into a functional one? I will take that up in the next chapter.

4

ROOTS OF THE MODERN ETHOS

A people's value system is a continuum, and so the ultimate source of contemporary values lies shrouded somewhere in the mythological age. Still, there are limits to how far back one can look and still discern values that bear any resemblance to those of the present day. Values are a function of conditions, and conditions in ancient times were markedly different from today. To discover the source of contemporary Japanese values, we really need look no further than the Tokugawa, or Edo, period (1603–1868).

The Tokugawa period was a postwar era of sorts, preceded by almost three hundred years of social, economic, and political turmoil that culminated in an unsuccessful attempt to invade Korea—a prelude, as it were, to our disastrous experience in World War II. With the establishment of the Tokugawa shogunate, the country entered a period of prosperity and order. Values suited to times of war naturally gave way to peacetime values.

Tokugawa Heritage

In many ways the Tokugawa period is the most interesting in Japan's history. During that time Japan developed a truly independent social system, one that remained largely unchanged for nearly three hundred years. It was not an age of imitation like the Meiji period, when we emulated the West, or like the postwar years, when America became our model. Nor was it like the classical period, when we patterned our culture after a Chinese model. In a sense it might be called our most original age. Tokugawa thinkers had to rely on their own resources, while politicians groped toward a new order by trial and error. The new system was built on the base of the indigenous value system and the social structure that supported it.

The Tokugawa period can be roughly divided in two, with 1710 as the rough line of demarcation. The first half may be considered a continuation of the Momoyama period (1573–1603). Order was established, political and economic systems were set in place, and the country entered a period of rapid economic growth. In the latter half the system appears to stagnate, but, in fact, during this time education spread, popular culture developed, and the standard of living for the masses rose. The country seemed to be gathering energy for the plunge into the Meiji period. Not only did Tokugawa society have much in common with modern Japan; it is the base on which modern Japanese society was built.

It is usual to think of the Tokugawa period as characterized by the strict differentiation of the populace into the four classes of warrior, farmer, artisan, and merchant, but the distinction was not always clear-cut. In the case of Ishida Baigan (1685–1744), the focus of our attention in this chapter, his family was originally of the warrior class but they later became farmers. Though born a peasant, Baigan went into service as an apprentice in Kyoto, thereby becoming a member of the merchant class. This was a common practice for the second and third sons of

peasant families. Upward mobility was possible too; some bought their way into the warrior class. The fact that social mobility was possible indicates that all classes shared certain norms.

The social order and system of values that took shape in the Tokugawa period are prototypes of Japan's modern pseudo-consanguineous system, described in the previous chapter. In Tokugawa society, loyalty and filial piety were really one and the same; the consanguineous principle of filial piety was extended to cover all institutions. But before this was possible, a pseudo-consanguineous system had to have been established and functioning like the real thing, bringing nonconsanguineous groups together as if they were blood-related, creating fictive, main family-branch family relationships. Moreover, people had to have accepted the pseudo-consanguineous principle. (Only with this Tokugawa heritage could modern companies, their primary and secondary subsidiaries, be tied together in a familial relationship in the absence of blood ties or contracts.)

Ishida Baigan

Ishida Baigan is a representative figure from the latter half of the Tokugawa period who exerted great influence on the development of the value system that grew up in response to the new social structure. He is remembered today as the founder of the influential Ishida school of popular ethics (Sekimon Shingaku). Most of his career was spent as a diligent employee, not unlike his modern counterparts. It is primarily in his latter role that we will study Baigan. Owning to bad luck and the nature of his times, rather than lack of ability or flaws in his character, Baigan was never a very successful wage-earner. On this point, too, he resembles many modern salaried workers.

Baigan's life is described in *Ishida sensei jiseki* (The achievement of Master Ishida), the work of a disciple. He was born in 1685 in a mountain hamlet located about ten kilometers south of Kameoka station on the San'in Line. Now part of Kameoka city, Kyoto prefecture, it was called Tōge village in his day. Today it seems an out-of-the-way place, but because walking was the usual mode of transportation in the Tokugawa period, the village was in fact convenient to both Osaka and Kyoto.

Baigan's family was what we would call today a typical middle-class farming family. Situated in the mountains, their village had little land for cultivation. Its inhabitants eked out an existence mainly by farming and lumbering. Although Baigan's family was part of the Ishida clan, which had founded the village, life was never easy. He had an older brother and a younger sister, and there, too, his was a typical family. Being the second-born son, he had a relatively unpressured childhood. Moreover, he appears to have been an average boy in most respects; there are no episodes that presaged his genius, nor is there any record of his having had an education for precocious children.

Originally, the Ishida clan were minor local lords who held three villages in the area, but as a result of a political struggle, they lost their claim to their holdings and were reduced to working the land. This occurred a hundred years before Baigan's birth. Although his family was regarded as a branch of the Ishida clan, in reality they were clan retainers and had no blood ties with the main family. In a system prevalent at the time, known as *kabuuchi*, they were conferred honorary membership in the Ishida clan and were allowed to use its name as a reward for years of faithful service. The clan was a good example of a pseudo-consanguineous group centered on the main house.

The *kabuuchi* system survives today in the form of the corporate stock-sharing plan. Just as loyal retainers in Baigan's day were rewarded with honorary membership in the clan they served, so employees today are given shares of company stock, which heightens the workers' sense of membership in the collective group and promotes a strong sense of loyalty. This arrangement, of course, contrasts sharply with stockholding in a contractual society. There, whether one holds stock in one's own company or in another, it is an investment and nothing more.

Mountain Chestnuts

An anecdote recounted in *Ishida sensei jiseki* is of some interest, for it sheds light on Baigan's character, as well as the norms under which he and other Japanese lived.

One morning when Baigan was ten he went off to play in the mountains near his home. When he returned at lunchtime he showed his father five or six chestnuts he had picked up. His father asked him where he had found them, and Baigan replied that they had been lying on the boundary line between their own and their neighbor's mountain. In that case, said his father, they must belong to the neighbor, for none of their chestnut trees overhung the boundary line. Though Baigan had not yet finished his lunch, his father ordered him to go right away and put the chestnuts back where he had found them. Baigan did as he was told. Later in life he is said to have remarked, "I didn't really want to take the chestnuts back; it seemed a waste. At first I resented my father. I realize now it was for my own good."

Baigan's father was by no means atypical of Tokugawa peasants. As this episode shows, he perhaps had a clear idea of ownership, and the agricultural community's rules governing interpersonal relations were very strict in those days. Such was the society into which Baigan was born.

At the age of eleven, Baigan was sent to Kyoto as an apprentice (*detchi*). Apprentices were provided with food, clothing, and shelter, but received no wages. Sometimes they had to have rice sent from home, a custom that survived into this century. In many ways his apprentice period was similar to the time young workers now spend in company schools. Like students doing part-time work while they study, the apprentices did odd jobs and assisted the shop master, and in the process they acquired business and technical skills. It was an advantageous arrangement for both master and apprentice.

Workers generally became apprentices between the ages of eleven and fourteen. In so doing they became apprentice adults; though expected to behave like adults, they were not burdened with adult responsibilities. After several years of learning the trade, an apprentice became a worker and advanced to the rank of *tedai*, then *yadoiri*, and finally he established his own business or a subsidiary.

Unfortunately for Baigan, his career did not go so smoothly. Though once a man of means, his employer began to have business troubles at about the time Baigan went to work for him. Apprentices customarily received livery twice a year—at Bon and New Year—but Baigan's employer was unable even to provide these. When Baigan returned to his parents' home for a visit wearing the same clothes he had worn when he left four or five years earlier, Baigan's mother was understandably surprised. She asked him why, but he would not give her a straight answer. This was probably the reason why the friend of Baigan's father who had arranged the job in Kyoto later paid a call on the shop. Realizing that the company was on the verge of bankruptcy, he explained the situation to Baigan's father. He apologized profusely, and recommended that Baigan look for a more suitable place to work. Baigan's father, however, decided to have the boy return home.

When he finally returned, Baigan's mother asked him why he had tolerated such conditions without a word of complaint. She felt sorry for her serious son, and probably believed that had he mentioned the problem when he was home before, they might have been able to help. But when Baigan left home, he had been told to think of his master as both father and employer and to serve him faithfully, and this he had done. When you think of someone as your father, he is said to have replied, you don't go telling outsiders about his faults. It is not clear what his parents said in response to this but they probably had no answer. Today, too, sometimes a company employee commits suicide to protect company secrets; Baigan's loyalty was no less than that.

Baigan was raised in a village that was part of a pseudo-consanguineous clan centered on the Ishida family, and he himself was a member of the clan community. When he went into service in Kyoto, it was under a similar pseudo-consanguineous arrangement. The moment Baigan entered the company community of his employer, he automatically ceased to be a member of his clan community. Thus it was easy for him to think of his employer as his father.

Boom and Bust

The Tokugawa clan's victory over the Toyotomi clan in 1603 brought nearly three hundred years of civil war to a close. The first hundred years of the Tokugawa period were really postwar years, because they were a period of recovery. As in the twenty-five years after World War II, when many small and medium-sized enterprises throughout the country grew into large industries almost overnight, the Japanese economy grew very rapidly during the early Tokugawa period.

The feudalistic system founded by the Tokugawas established the above-mentioned four classes, clearly dividing society by occupation. Though formally at the bottom of the social ladder, the merchant class was by far the most vigorous, leading the populist educator Honda Toshiaki (1744–1821) to comment, "To all outward appearances this country is ruled by the warrior class, but, in reality, it is ruled by merchants." The author of *Seken kenbunroku* (A record of worldly happenings) notes, "More than anyone else, merchants are free to make profits, indulge their desires, and work as they please. Unaffected by wind, water, or drought, exempted from the land tax and public service, they enjoy more freedom than any other class." Indeed, the freedom of warriors was restricted by the lord-vassal relationship; that of farmers by dependence on the land, submission to the feudalistic system, and vulnerability to the vagaries of the weather; and that of artisans by the level of their craft and skill. But a merchant's potential for making profits, indulging his desires, and working as he pleased in free competition with others was limited only by his ability.

Every merchant belonged to a collective body whose function was the pursuit of commerce. To say that merchants were free to work as they pleased is to say that those who worked hardest were the most prosperous. One's fate was intertwined with that of one's business. To survive amid the keen competition of the time, a business had to be a functional unit, and to function effectively its members had to possess prodigious diligence and self-control.

By Baigan's generation, however, the economic boom was over. No longer did workers uniformly move up the seniority ladder, guaranteed eventually to be established on their own, as retired workers of modern times are given positions in subsidiaries. In many ways the economic situation resembled that of today, when growth has come to a standstill.

They were bad economic times when Baigan, at the age of twenty-three, once more went into service in Kyoto, probably for a dry-goods dealer named Kuroyanagi. Although he could not have counted on smooth advancement through the seniority system, if Baigan had entered the company in his teens as an apprentice he would at least have had a chance for promotion. But by entering ten years late, he found himself outside the seniority system altogether. Because the average lifespan in those days was fifty years, and workers commonly retired at forty-five, his experience was comparable to entering a company at thirty-five today.

It is apparent from Baigan's writings and from anecdotes about him that he was an extemely honest, ingenuous person. He once described himself as a "creature of logic." His own description seems most apt, as is apparent from his work *Tohi mondō* (Town and country: questions and answers). As the title suggests, it is written in question-and-answer form; Baigan is supposedly responding to questions asked by someone else, but more likely the question-answer form is his own invention, by which he hoped to refute or revise statements he had made himself. At one point the questioner asks Baigan his opinion of the story of creation as recorded in the *Kojiki* and *Nihon shoki*, Japan's oldest surviving prose works, asserting that it must be a fabrication. If man had been created after the formation of heaven and earth, the questioner argues, there would have been no one present to witness the event. Baigan agrees. Baigan's determination to think things through logically is striking. I know of no one, even as late as the World War II years, who declared the story of Japan's creation to be a myth using a similar logic.

His strict self-control and habit of subjecting everything to methodical reasoning made Baigan somewhat inflexible, yet extremely reliable, as an employee. Though he realized he was trapped in a dead-end job, he refused to indulge himself in dissipation or amusement. As a result, he soon displayed symptoms of neurosis and his work began to suffer.

Worried about Baigan, the mother of his employer and the shop's head clerk suggested that he visit the gay quarters. Today one would be told to go to a cabaret. Baigan considered their words: If he did as they suggested, his employer would have to bear the expense; this was not right. Yet the alternative was to continue as he was, taking medicine day and night, for which his employer was also paying. At last he decided that it was in his employer's best interests for him to visit the pleasure district. For a time Baigan gave himself to dissipation.

But it was not a long-term solution. He soon recovered from his depression and could no longer claim that his dissipation was for his employer's sake; plainly it was for his own pleasure. This amounted to stealing from the man. When he realized this, he felt worse than before. He immediately explained the situation to his employer, sold some of his clothing and his short sword, and paid him back. His is the kind of story one would like to share with the many Japanese executives today who are dubbed *shayōzoku* (the expense account tribe).

Free Thinker

To what can we attribute Baigan's manner of thinking? Undeniably his character, his childhood education, and his immediate environment were all contributing factors. An especially important influence was the age in which he grew up, an age of enlightenment, when knowledge was made available to the masses through books known as *kanazōshi*. Clearly the enlightenment atmosphere did much to stimulate the logical, intellectually curious Baigan. *Kanazōshi* is a broad genre—so broad that the term "genre" is misleading. It embraces everything from adult comic books to enlightenment and didactic works. Many resemble modern "how to" books, offering practical advice on tea ceremony, flower arranging, cooking, etiquette, ballad singing, and the like. Others present fascinating discussions of Confucianism and Buddhism. Today these works would be touted as "upholding the highest standards of scholarship, yet easily understood by the layman."

Baigan was a compulsive reader. While serving his master as both clerk and salesman, it is said that he was never without a book. He read in the middle of a sale, he got up early to read before work, and he read late into the night. It is not clear what kind of books he read, but judging from the erudition of his later writings, despite the lack of formal education, it seems safe to conclude that his reading ranged over the entire *kanazōshi* genre. In a word, he internalized the plebeian intellectual milieu in which he lived.

One need not search for the source of Baigan's thinking; his thoughts were his own. More than anything else, he was a clerk in a store, not a representative of some school of thought. If we had to describe Baigan in his later years, we would probably say he was a sort of townsman-Confucian, what might today be called a social commentator, and nothing more—certainly not a bona fide scholar with the appropriate credentials. He continued to study for his entire life, and his reading was by no means confined to *kanazōshi*, but the basis of his thinking throughout his life remained plebeian and wholly his own.

Like all writing of the day, Baigan's works are studded with quotations from Shintō, Confucian, and Buddhist sources. Sometimes they are offered as the wisdom of the sages. In most cases, however, quotations are used arbitrarily, not necessarily as their authors intended. Baigan would ignore the context of the passage he quoted, borrowing its literal meaning to advance his own argument. The original framework of ideas was broken up and individual ideas incorporated piecemeal into an intellectual matrix of his own creation. Therefore, whatever the source, and however long the quotation, each must be regarded as the thought of Baigan.

Being a merchant, Baigan was thoroughly rational. To function as such, one needed to be rational where money was concerned, rational by nature. Rationality is in highest demand in times of economic stagnation, rather than during an economic boom. Until the 1970s, when we were disabused of the myth of unlimited economic growth potential and we abandoned our grandiose plan to "remodel the Japanese archipelago," we believed that any enterprise would succeed. The same was true of the early Tokugawa period. But about the time of the shogun Yoshimune's reforms in the Kyōhō period, the illusion was shattered.

The Kyōhō reforms centered on the shogunate and the warrior class. Civil administration, as practiced from the time of Tsunayoshi and Ieharu, was discredited, and instead the government encouraged simplicity and frugality, prohibited extravagance, and promoted the martial arts. It also attempted to promote industry, but this went no further than physiocracy, which mainly benefited the warrior class.

One result was stagnation in the economy, business, and industry, but it also gave rise to the argument that merchants are unnecessary, which resembles the thinking among some today that general trading houses (*sōgō shōsha*) are basically evil. Actually human thinking changes little over the ages. When business prospers, merchants are valued, but when times are bad they are often made out to be more corrupt than the politicians who siphon off their meager profits.

This atmosphere led Baigan to comment, "People accuse only the merchants of being greedy and unprincipled, caring only for profit. People resent their activities and would like to curtail them. Why are merchants singled out?" If one looks at the rabidly antimerchant writings of Ogyū Sorai, Hayashi Shihei, and Takano Shōseki, one can understand what he was speaking of.

Meanwhile merchants themselves began to give consideration to their proper role in society, as would anyone who pursues his thoughts to their logical conclusion. This produced works like Nishikawa Joken's *Chōnin bukuro* (The merchant's purse) and Mitsui Takafusa's *Chōnin kōkenroku* (A merchant's observations). There is little doubt that these works exerted a profound influence on the rational, introverted Baigan. In his own writings, he went on to explore the ideal role of man in society and how he himself could conform to this ideal.

Someone who shared lodgings with Baigan was amazed at his reading habits. Why, he asked, do you crave knowledge? Baigan replied that he did not seek knowledge in itself, but that through study he hoped to profit from the wisdom of the sages and thus discover the ideal state for man. He sought to become this sort of man himself and to be a model for others, he said. Throughout his life, Baigan disliked those who prided themselves on their learning, contemptuously referring to them as *moji geisha* (learned geisha). No doubt he sensed a danger in the argument that merchants served no purpose, and he was wary of merchants' irrationality, which was partly to blame for the sentiment against them at the time. Thus he said, "Though I may be wandering about the town ringing a bell that no one can hear, I must try to show them the Way." In order to find "the Way" and to pass the wisdom on to mankind, Baigan avidly read and lived according to a strict code of personal behavior.

Though Baigan was highly individualistic, he did not live in a vacuum. Like all thinkers, he was heir to an intellectual heritage. To whom, then, was he most indebted? It seems that at about thirty-five Baigan believed he understood the proper way for man to live, but that the realization unnerved him. For six months to a year he sought teaching from a number of Confucianists, but was unable to pick up anything useful.

At about this time, he met Oguri Ryōun and became his pupil. Concerning Ryōun, we know only that he was originally of the warrior class and that he studied Zen. Under Ryōun, Baigan seems to have undergone an intellectual awakening when he was told, "Man is by nature indiscriminate." Because a *kanazōshi* of unknown authorship called *Menashigusa* (Indiscriminate grass) was popular at the time, it is surmised that it strongly influenced Baigan.

However, part of *Menashigusa* is titled "Ninin bikuni" (Two nuns), the same as a work by Suzuki Shōsan, whom we will discuss in the next chapter. It is thought possible that the volume is Shōsan's creation or that he wrote it based on another, probably earlier, work. It would seem, therefore, either that Baigan was the inheritor of the ideas of Shōsan or that both men are indebted to the same source. In either case, they were very close in their thinking, as was noted by one of Baigan's disciples in his preface to a work by Shōsan.

Ryōun died in 1729 at the age of sixty. Apparently, Baigan was his most trusted disciple and logical successor, for just before his death he told Baigan that he could have all the works he had annotated. Receiving one's teacher's library is considered a great honor even today, but in the Tokugawa period, when the secret teachings of masters were valued above all else, it meant no less than that Baigan had been chosen to succeed Ryōun. Baigan, however, curtly replied that he did not want the library. When Ryōun asked why, he said that he was certain to put his own interpretation to the works. Ryōun was reportedly delighted with his response. Indeed, it seems very much in character. For while Baigan read widely and was devoted to Ryōun, he remained strongly individualistic and supremely self-confident. Above all else, he wanted to think for himself and to give expression to his own ideas.

After Ryōun's death, Baigan quit his job and opened a small, private school. This was the start of what came to be known throughout Japan as Sekimon Shingaku, which was to have a profound influence in Japan.

Basis for Capitalism

Had Baigan been a salaried worker in Japan today, he would have been a splendid one. In any advanced nation, a person like Baigan would be considered a dependable businessman. An especially significant aspect of Baigan's thinking is his starkly clear conception of private ownership. Without a clear conception of private ownership, capitalism could not have developed in Japan. As we have seen, the concept existed in rural villages at the time, but Baigan developed it further. Many years after he paid his employer back for the money he spent in the gay quarters, Baigan wrote, "What is mine is mine, what is not is not. I intend to be repaid all I have lent others and to pay back all that I have borrowed. This goes for everything—even a strand of hair. There is no other way to live honestly."

Not all nations understand the idea of private ownership. As the Kremlinologist Shimizu Hayao points out, this concept is lacking in the Soviet Union. When Russians have something, they share it among themselves. When they are without, they think nothing of stealing from others. Needless to say, differing conceptions of ownership can lead to serious misunderstandings.

What made possible the appearance of someone like Baigan? In the age of warring states, the average citizen did not think as he did. The age as it is portrayed in medieval literature is totally different from the world of Baigan. People then showed none of Baigan's self-restraint. Robbery was a part of everyday life. But in the early Tokugawa period, norms underwent a sudden and dramatic change. Not everyone in the Tokugawa period shared the intensity of Baigan's sense of right and wrong, but it is clear that his were essentially the norms of the time. This is the age that produced Japanese whom we can finally recognize as resembling Japanese of today.

No matter how much wealth a nation might accumulate, how much oil it might possess, it cannot modernize without undergoing the same degree of change in societal norms. Once the change has occurred, even if it is bereft of all wealth and natural resources and forced to start from scratch, like Japan after World War II, a nation can modernize.

But what triggered this crucial change? It was not the Protestant ethic or a mercantile morality based on it. In the next chapter we will explore what it was that set the stage for Ishida Baigan's appearance and propelled Japan along the road to modernization.

5

ZEN AND THE ECONOMIC
ANIMAL

The effect of a man's thought on later generations, especially when it is progressive or highly original, is rarely what he expects it will be. Were Jesus to visit the Vatican today and see the mammoth institution that has grown from the seeds of his teaching, he might well disavow it. If Karl Marx could inspect the "Gulag Archipelago" and if he were told that its facilities are the product of his thinking, he would not hesitate to separate himself from it entirely. The same is true of religious reformers. If John Calvin were shown America's capitalistic society and told that it is the fruit of the Protestant ethic, he would probably be rendered speechless. A thought system functions in a variety of ways at a certain time within a given social context, but society itself does not change in exact conformity with the directions of that thought. Yet among the thinker's original ideas, one can often identify the seeds of later social change.

In this chapter we will examine the thinking of the man whom I see as most directly responsible for the development of capitalism in Japan, Suzuki Shōsan. No doubt Shōsan also would be dumbfounded to hear himself labeled the father of Japanese capitalism. Certainly, he did not foresee present-day Japanese society, or even the flour-ishing merchant culture of the Genroku through the Kyōhō periods (1688–1735). Had someone explained to that staid Zen monk the effect his thought would have on Japanese society, surely he would have been appalled. Some of his followers today might take exception as well.

Unique Zen Philosopher

In the circumstances of his life and in his character, Suzuki Shōsan differed greatly from Ishida Baigan, whose youth and career were discussed in the last chapter, and whose philosophy will be taken up in the next. Shōsan's lifetime spanned the close of the turbulent Sengoku period and the era of the fourth Tokugawa shogun, Ietsuna (r. 1651–80). The changes that occurred in his life mirrored the times.

A samurai from Mikawa (present-day Aichi prefecture), Shōsan was a retainer of Tokugawa Ieyasu, and he took part in the fighting that brought nearly three centuries of civil war to a close and led to the establishment of the Tokugawa shogunate. After peace was restored, Shōsan worked for a time as a shogunate official in Osaka. Then, in 1620, for reasons known only to himself, he suddenly took the tonsure. He was aware that his action violated shogunate law and that the authorities might expropriate his entire assets and discontinue the family line, ordering him to commit ritual suicide. Fortunately they did not, and Shōsan lived to the ripe old age of seventy-seven as a Zen monk, and a most extraordinary one at that.

Interestingly, the times in which Shōsan lived resembled the era of Baigan in one important respect: a large segment of the population had lost sight of their reason for living.

Just as society in Baigan's day struggled to adapt to a stagnant economy after years of prosperity, society in Shōsan's day had to adjust to peace after years of civil war. Certainly many people welcomed peace; even samurai, to some extent, had had enough of civil disorder, but the establishment of a peaceful social order deprived the warrior of his raison d'être. Gone were the days when a peasant might rise to the foremost position of power through his martial exploits, as Toyotomi Hideyoshi had done. After the third shogun, Iemitsu, it was clear that a coup d'état against the shogunate was out of the question. Many samurai remained thwarted, feeling useless. It may be that a sense of frustration prompted Shōsan to become a priest. How to resolve the contradiction—to find a reason for living in a new social environment—was the challenge Shōsan and others of his generation faced.

The biggest problem one encounters when dealing with a Japanese thinker is the lack of systematization of his ideas. Christianity has a systematic, organized theology, enabling one to consider the interrelation of religion and society within the theme of Christian social ethics. But in the case of Zen, there is no such systematic "theology," or body of religious thought. Organization is anathema to Zen.

Strangely enough, we find in the writings of Shōsan something like a systematic Zen "theology," as well as a corresponding Zen social ethic. Shōsan once remarked, "I would like to see the world governed by Buddhist laws." Though he took Buddhist orders, he by no means abandoned the world, but remained keenly interested in politics and society throughout his life. On this point alone we must surely call him a unique Zen thinker.

Perhaps the reason for the systematic approach in Shōsan's thinking is the fact that he was an anti-Christian ideologue, which is clear from his work *Hakirishitan* (Debunking the Christian myth), partly a Zen rebuttal to Christian teachings. To challenge another philosophical system, there is no choice but to turn the logic in it against itself. To do this you must arrange your own argument in contraposition to the other.

In most cultures philosophies take shape in a dialectical process of this kind, but in Japan's case there have been few opportunities for polemics and debate. This goes for the modern period as well, for imitation, our modern forte, does not admit debate. One result is that Japanese have lost their powers of self-expression, the ability to communicate not only with the outside world but among themselves as well. For this reason they do not understand themselves.

The Buddhist Trinity

In *Hakirishitan,* Shōsan defines the essence of the cosmos as the Buddha. This Buddha-nature cannot be seen or perceived, but it possesses three "virtues" that affect mankind, thus attesting to its existence. The three virtues he calls the Moon, the Heart, and the Great Healing King, by which he refers to three aspects of the Buddha, not three separate buddhas. His conceptualization clearly corresponds to Trinitarianism.

The Moon stands for the cosmos, the natural order. In the same way that a reflection of the moon's essence dwells within a drop of water, the Moon, the natural order, resides within every person's heart. This is the virtue of the Heart. Because humans are a part of the cosmos, their nature conforms to the cosmic order, and they need merely do as the heart commands. Naturally the concept of a holistic order is not Shōsan's alone; it is found in medieval Christian thought and in the doctrines of Chu-tzû. It is one of the fundamental ideas in the intellectual history of mankind.

If every man has a Buddha-nature, there should be no war, no crime, no injustice; all people should behave like a Buddha. Why, then, did Japan suffer through nearly three hundred years of civil war? This is a question that preoccupied all Japanese thinkers of Shōsan's day. In Shōsan's opinion, the mind, like the body, fell victim to disease. All grief, he believed, was caused by three "poisons": greed, anger, and discontent. The mind's illnesses could be treated by the Great Healing King; to beg for a cure was to demonstrate one's faith. And if all people were cured and lived in accordance with the dictates of the Heart, there would be no more war and all social problems would disappear. They would live together harmoniously, each as a living Buddha, in a utopian society.

In Shōsan's view, to build a good society the heart of man first had to be protected from the three poisons. This required one to "become a Buddha," by which he meant to live in accordance with the dictates of the Heart. One had to engage in ascetic exercise, that is, Buddhist practice, to live this way, but how? Unlike priests, who were free to spend their days in ascetic practice, the average person had to work hard and steadily just to earn a living. How could they be saved? Shōsan's answer: Everyday labor was Buddhist practice if performed with the right intention. With this conception as a base, he formulated what must be called a Zen social ethic, a concrete guide to how man should live. As such, its effect reached far beyond the sphere of religion to affect the whole of secular society.

Work Equals Asceticism

Shōsan presents his social ethic in *Shimin nichiyō* (Daily life for the four classes). Like Baigan's *Tohi mondō*, it is written in question-and-answer form. Representatives of each class—samurai, farmer, artisan, and merchant—ask Shōsan how they should live, and he explains. *Shimin nichiyō* was later combined with *Sanbō tokuyō* (The three precious virtues) to form the work entitled *Banmin tokuyō* (Virtues of all), which Shōsan's disciple Keichū called his most important tract. It is possible that Shōsan became a monk so that he could spread the teachings embodied in this work. Because I believe *Shimin nichiyō* is the key to understanding Shōsan's philosophy, let us briefly examine its content.

In the section on farmers, a peasant asks, "We are taught that the next life (life after death) is important and that we should not spare ourselves in Buddhist practice, but farm work keeps us so busy we do not have any time for practice. How unfair it seems that simply because we must make a living through menial labor, we are destined to waste this life and suffer in the next. How can we attain Buddhahood?" Shōsan's answer is admirably clear: agricultural labor is Buddhist practice. It is a mistake, he says, to take time out from one's labor to pray for rebirth in Paradise. Agricultural labor itself is ascetic exercise.

> You must toil in extremes of heat and cold, spade, hoe, and sickle in hand. Your mind and body overgrown with the thicket of desire is your enemy. Torture yourself—plow, reap—work with all your heart. . . . When one is unoccupied, the thicket of desire grows, but when one toils, subjecting one's mind and body to pain, one's heart is at peace. In this way one is engaged in Buddhist practice all the time. Why should a peasant long for another road to Buddhahood?

A peasant who followed Shōsan's advice was far more exalted than the most virtuous of priests, since priests did almost no work at all. It was a question of the frame of mind in which one worked, not the kind of work one did.

If a farmer treats his work as asceticism, not only will he achieve Buddhahood but society will be purified. Shōsan explains it like this:

> Your birth as a farmer is Heaven's gift to the world, your mission being to nurture the world's people. Therefore, give yourself wholeheartedly to the way of Heaven with no thought for yourself. Serve Heaven through your farm labors. Celebrate the gods and Buddhas by raising the five grains, and save the people. Make a solemn vow to administer even to insects. Chant *namu Amida butsu* with each stroke of your hoe. Work earnestly, and with each stroke of your sickle your fields will be purified. The five grains will then become pure food that will work as medicine to extinguish the desires of those who eat it.

In Shōsan's thinking, to work with all one's heart led to enlightenment and to freedom from all earthly constraints, making one a living Buddha. Work itself was ascetic practice. This concept forms the basis of Shōsan's social ethic.

Japanese Religiosity

Next an artisan poses the following question. "I am busy every minute of the day in an effort to earn my livelihood. How can I become a Buddha?" Shōsan answers:

> All occupations are Buddhist practice; through work we are able to attain Buddhahood. There is no calling that is not Buddhist. All is for the good of the world. . . . The all-encompassing Buddha-nature manifest in us all works for the world's good:

without artisans, such as the blacksmith, there would be no tools; without officials there would be no order in the world; without farmers there would be no food; without merchants we would suffer inconvenience. All the other occupations as well are for the good of the world. . . . All reveal the blessing of the Buddha. Those who are ignorant of the blessing of our Buddha-nature, who do not value themselves and their innate Buddha-nature and fall into evil ways of thinking and behaving, have lost their way.

Because all human beings possess a Buddha-nature, to become Buddhas,

> Above all you must believe in yourself. If you truly desire to become a Buddha, just believe in yourself. Believing in yourself is believing in the Buddha, for the Buddha is in you. The Buddha has no desires, its heart contains no anger, no discontent, no life or death . . . no right or wrong . . . no passions . . . no evil. . . .

Finally he says, "Believe with all your heart. Believe." Faith to Shōsan was faith in oneself; there is no absolute, monotheistic god in Shōsan's conception. Yet his exhortation to believe in oneself was not, of course, a defense of vanity.

An understanding of Shōsan's approach to religion gives us valuable insight into modern Japanese society. It is commonly asserted that the Japanese are not a religious people, but this is shockingly untrue. Only the nature of our faith differs from that of Christians or Moslems. In Japan it is the Buddha of the Heart rather than God in whom one believes and to whom one is held accountable for one's actions. A Japanese can say he has lost faith in God, and society will pay little attention, but let him say he has lost faith in himself and he will find that he has lost his credentials as a member of society, just as an apostate Christian or Moslem would elsewhere. In either case soci-

ety is understandably suspicious of one who believes that
one cannot be held accountable for one's actions.

Japanese themselves are guilty of perpetuating the myth
that they are not religious. From the middle of the Tokugawa period, Confucian influence strongly colored the
daily vocabulary. Then in the early Meiji period there
arose an anti-Buddhist movement, which led the government to order all Buddhist expressions deleted from the
state-controlled textbooks. For this reason Japanese no
longer appreciate the religious meaning of the words they
use. Expressions people use all the time, such as "I must
have been out of my mind" (*Jibun ga shinjirarenai,* lit., "I
cannot believe myself") or "To be honest with you"
(*Honshin dewa,* lit., "In my heart of hearts"), are actually
expressions of religious ideas. Because Japanese are not
aware of the religious implications of the words they use,
they do not see how deeply religion is still a part of their
life and thought.

Pilgrim's Progress

The next section of *Shimin nichiyō* describes how merchants ought to live. In countries everywhere, merchants
tend to be regarded with condescension or disfavor. In
Tokugawa Japan, this tendency was especially strong, particularly among samurai. Shōsan, however, does not show
the least contempt for commerce or the merchants who
practice it.

In Shōsan's view, "Commerce is the function Heaven
has assigned to those whose job it is to promote freedom
throughout the country." Today we use the word "freedom" in a variety of ways, tending to forget that one basic
freedom is the free access to goods. Without the distribu-

tion of goods through commerce our freedom would be impaired in countless ways. Far from holding merchants in contempt, Shōsan valued them for the vital function they perform. Considering the time in which he lived and his samurai origins, Shōsan's enlightened thinking was unusual indeed.

While Shōsan considers commerce, like all occupations, to be a godly activity, he does not value commerce in itself as much as the way it is performed—whether or not it is performed as Buddhist practice. A merchant asks, "I ceaselessly pursue my humble trade in hopes of realizing a profit, but to my great regret I will never be able to achieve Buddhahood. Please tell me the way." In his answer, Shōsan would by no means deny the merchant his profit, but he would urge him first to cultivate through asceticism the sort of attitude that will bring about profits: an unbendable commitment to honesty.

Honesty is an essential element in Shōsan's philosophy. If as a merchant you realize that your job is to bring freedom to the nation and unfailingly "pursue your calling with honesty, just as fire burns and water flows downhill, so the blessings of Heaven will follow and your every wish will be fulfilled." Yet one must not delight in realizing a profit. Such behavior Shōsan calls "illusory goodness." To be content only after taking a profit encourages vanity and is sure to lead one into evil ways. Real goodness is non-illusory; one must engage in commerce with no illusions.

Shōsan provides the following concrete advice for merchants:

> Throw yourself headlong into worldly activity. For the sake of the nation and its citizens, send the goods of your province to other provinces, and bring the products of other provinces into your own. Travel around the country to distant parts to bring

people what they desire. Your activity is an ascetic exercise that will cleanse you of all impurities. Challenge your mind and body by crossing mountain ranges. Purify your heart by fording rivers. When your ship sets sail on the boundless sea, lose yourself in prayer to the Buddha. If you understand that this life is but a trip through an evanescent world, and if you cast aside all attachments and desires and work hard, Heaven will protect you, the gods will bestow their favor, and your profits will be exceptional. You will become a person of wealth and virtue and care nothing for riches. Finally you will develop an unshakable faith; you will be engaged in meditation around the clock.

To achieve Buddhahood a merchant must travel around the provinces distributing goods as if on a pilgrimage.

Zen Social Ethic

In Shōsan's conception, then, worldly labor is religious asceticism, and if one pursues a calling—any calling—with singleminded devotion one can become a Buddha. This is Shōsan's cardinal principle. Agriculture is Buddhist practice; by earnestly working the land, not only does a peasant become a Buddha himself, but the whole society is purified. If an artisan devotes himself to his calling, goods will be produced in limitless quantity for the benefit of the world. This, too, is the blessing of the Buddha, and the artisans possess a Buddha-nature. Merchants, by satisfying the demand for goods, bring comfort and convenience to the populace while achieving Buddhahood for themselves. In the section "The Desire for Asceticism, the Virtue or the Three Treasures, and Everyday Life for the Samurai," he sums it up: "Because secular law is Buddhist law . . . it is reasonable that by following worldly law you can attain Buddhahood. . . . If you fail to use worldly law to attain

Buddhahood. . . . If you fail to use worldly law to attain Buddhahood, then you know nothing of the will of the Buddha. It is your will that changes secular law into Buddhist law."

Shōsan's concept is truly unique, yet it is based on Zen. Among samurai of the time, swordsmanship and Zen were considered one and the same. A samurai continually polished his skill with the sword, not to increase his ability to fight but because it was considered a form of Zen asceticism. Shōsan's genius was in expanding this concept to the other three classes. As such, his philosophy might be called a Zen social ethic based on systematic Zen "theology."

The times in which Shōsan lived surely played a part in the formation of his thinking. As explained above, society had moved from a time of civil disorder to one of peace and stability. Although order had been established and the people lived in peace, they were forced to abandon glorious dreams of great achievements and riches. As society gradually settled into the firm pattern of four classes, many people lost sight of their reason for living. Shōsan sought to resolve their distress by finding a spiritual meaning in everyday labor, and to this end, he expounded his ideas widely. He said that he wished to conquer the world with Buddhist law; his immediate goal was the establishment of a system based on the social ethic described above. He envisioned his social ethic becoming a basis for order, a sort of national morality by which people would achieve a spiritual, even religious satisfaction.

Shōsan's ideas are strikingly modern. Today it is easy to see how they could change attitudes toward work and provide an ethos for capitalism in Japan. Still, his philosophy has functioned in a variety of ways depending on the demands of the time. It can be interpreted as an affirmation of secular society, as was the philosophy of John Calvin, and this is exactly what happened. Shōsan argued that secular law was Buddhist law, but society interpreted his words to mean that Buddhist law was secular law.

Economic Animals or Zen Ascetics?

Today we still instinctually sense that it is wrong to seek profit, but that profits that naturally result from labor are acceptable, and this idea derives from Shōsan. For example, a department store will say in its advertisements, "Through and through, we are here to serve you." The founder/owner of a leading electronics maker is often quoted as saying that he never once worked to make a profit for his company, but that every effort he made throughout his career was to provide people with electrical and electronic products as cheaply as tapwater. Of course one might argue that if a business did nothing but serve society it would go broke in short order, and that companies are in business to make a profit; if they were not, they would not last long in the competitive business world of Japan. But this misses the point.

If one followed Shōsan's philosophy, however, one would conclude that because the department store was determined to provide the best service it could to its customers, it made a profit; were it to seek profits it would not only fail to realize them but might even go bankrupt. Because the electronics maker followed the dictates of the Heart, he was able to produce goods that benefited the world, and in the process he realized a profit. In Shōsan's words, "Those who care nothing for the people but think only of profit incur the wrath of Heaven, meet with misfortune, and are despised by all. If you do not love and respect everyone you will fail in everything you do." To apply Shōsan's advice and make Buddhist law the law of the world is the best business practice.

The same attitude is shared by Japanese salesmen abroad. Someone once remarked that Japanese salesmen trekking through the wilds of Africa look for all the world like pilgrims. In a sense they are pilgrims. They are following Shōsan's admonition to treat commerce as an ascetic exercise, like a pilgrimage. They are like Muslims making their way to Mecca, except that unlike the latter, their pilgrimage will bring their company a profit.

Zen enjoys tremendous popularity in the West these days. When I travel abroad I often find myself deluged with questions. To foreigners, Zen is mysterious and obscure, the very essence of the exotic East. Whenever I am asked to explain Zen, I reply that to understand Zen one should study Japan's large trading houses. I then proceed to describe Shōsan's *Shimin nichiyō,* explaining that to Japanese work is not an economic activity, but Zen ascetic exercise. I say that this spirit is behind Japan's image as a land of "economic animals." My listeners are always amazed. They never dreamed that the influence of Zen is still so pervasive, any more than the average American is consciously aware of the ubiquitous presence of Puritan traditions in his own society. It is the same in every society; a people's intellectual heritage is transformed in various ways in response to conditions, but remains fundamentally unchanged.

Despite the strong religious coloring of Japanese society, we might be said to be anticlerical. Shōsan's writings contain numerous statements critical of the priesthood as being unproductive. Indeed, if work itself is religious practice, what need has society for priests? Japanese respect one who exhibits a religious attitude toward work, yet they look askance at priests, and this attitude contributes to the mistaken impression that Japanese are an irreligious people. Because a person not engaged in productive labor is not engaged in ascetic exercise, Japanese regard such a person with the same suspicion as some Westerners do an atheist. For this reason Japanese dread retirement, an attitude that contrasts sharply with that of many Americans, who eagerly await retirement as a time of liberation.

Once, the Japanese penchant for work was attributed to the country's poverty. The fallacy of this theory is clear enough today, when Japan ranks among the world's most prosperous nations. If poverty made a people into hard workers, then the majority of the world's population should work far more diligently than Japanese. A religious attitude toward work, not poverty, is behind Japan's economic success.

When we have developed our economy sufficiently we will seek the way of the Buddha in other pursuits. No matter how we do it, we will continue to seek the way. And, as always, the inability to find it will be our greatest source of pain. It is this contradiction that gives rise to debate on the meaning of life. Shōsan's writings, too, reflect the same kind of philosophical considerations.

Shōsan's thought is an original Japanese philosophy developed during the Tokugawa period, when the people fashioned an independent social system with their own hands. Of course society did not develop along the lines that Shōsan envisioned. If he were shown Japanese society today and told that it is the result of his thinking, he might explode in anger. Nevertheless, there is no denying that his thought has lived on and has functioned in various ways. Let us summarize the basis of that thought.

The human heart and society must conform with the natural order. This requires all to follow the dictates of the Heart, that is, the cosmic order within oneself. Impediments to following the Heart are the three posions. To protect oneself from them, one must follow the Great Healing King and observe the established law of health, which calls on everyone to believe that his or her occupation is Buddhist practice and engage in it wholeheartedly. Work should be undertaken with an honest attitude. If everyone works diligently with this attitude, society, the sum of its individual parts, becomes a Buddha. At the same time, the products of that labor benefit society, and to distribute goods as if one were on a pilgrimage is to liberate everyone. Finally, a correspondence between the individual heart, society, and the cosmos will be achieved, people will enjoy spiritual satisfaction, and society will be free from disorder.

Between Shōsan and the present stands Ishida Baigan. His concern with honesty was stimulated by Shōsan, to whom we must attribute the emergence of people like Baigan in the middle Tokugawa period.

6

THEOLOGY AND JAPANESE PRAGMATISM

As we noted in the last chapter, Ishida Baigan in his intellectual growth was heavily indebted to Suzuki Shōsan. Yet his philosophy, which we will examine in this chapter, was unique in its time and broad enough that it speaks even to modern Japanese society.

At forty-two or -three Baigan left his employment as a clerk, and at forty-five he opened a small private academy in his home in Kurumaya-chō, Kyoto. At first, few took him seriously, as he was no more than an unknown, erstwhile clerk. Some dismissed him outright as uneducated, while others were outwardly respectful but ridiculed him behind his back. Only a handful were sincere in their praise—after all, he had almost no pupils and little to show for himself. But Baigan charged no fee for his teaching, and so it made no difference to him financially whether he had pupils or not. All he cared about was sharing with others the wisdom he believed he had obtained. Though he made no effort himself to attract more students, increasing numbers were drawn to his academy by word of mouth.

Japan's First Pragmatist

Baigan lectured every morning and every other night, and held seminars three times a month. His disciples were

91

mostly townspeople. Seven years after opening the academy, Baigan gave a month-long series of lectures in a large townhouse, and it is said that men and women flocked to hear him. Two years later, apparently because his Kuru-maya-chō house had grown too small, he moved to Sakai-chō. Now Baigan was often invited to give lectures in Osaka, as well as in Kyoto.

But it was still a small academy and remained so until two generations of Baigan's disciples had emerged. By then the Sekimon Shingaku* (Ishida school of popular ethics) had spread throughout the three largest cities of the time—Kyoto, Osaka, and Edo—and over most of Japan, and its basic philosophy was reaching even the samurai class and the nobility.

Clearly Baigan had developed an attractive practical philosophy and a basic world view that fit the needs and desires of his society. Baigan's world view was essentially the same as Shōsan's and that of most other Tokugawa period philosophers. He developed his concept of a holistic order—that the cosmic order, man's inner order, and the social order are and must be one and the same—from the teachings of Chu-tzu, and for this reason he expressed his ideas in Confucian terms. But because his world view and Shōsan's were fundamentally parallel, schematically they appear to be quite similar; it is usually possible to substitute Baigan's words for Shōsan's without any problem. In this sense, the differences between the thinking of the two men are largely differences in terminology.

In other ways, however, their thinking diverged. For example, Baigan clearly contradicted Shōsan when Baigan said, "To try to let Buddhist law govern worldly rules is as

---

*"Shingaku" means literally "study of the Heart." The name "Sekimon" consists of the first character of Ishida's surname, read "seki," and the character *mon*, literally meaning "gate."

wrong as trying to cross a river or the ocean on a horse or in a palanquin." In fact, one way to grasp Baigan's ideas is to compare his words with Shōsan's on certain teachings. To begin with, in Shōsan's conception the basis of the cosmos was the Buddha with three virtues: the Moon, the Buddha of the Heart, and the Great Healing King. Baigan called the basis of the cosmos "Goodness," and he posited three manifestations: "Heaven," "True Nature," and "Medicine."

As Baigan explains, Goodness does not imply the opposite of evil so much as the continuous order of the cosmos. Because this principle is manifested in Heaven as well as in human nature, it means that "human nature is basically good" in the sense that it is in harmony with the cosmos, with nature. In place of Shōsan's Great Healing King, he speaks of Medicine. In this he departs from Shōsan's more religious outlook, for "Medicine" implies something a person deliberately prepares and uses, instead of passively relying on the grace of a supernatural healing power.

To some extent, the difference between Shōsan and Baigan is the difference between a philosopher in a period of religious reform and a philosopher in a period of enlightenment. To Shōsan the cosmos was the Buddha, who was an anthropomorphic deity, and the Great Healing King was the savior. In Baigan's thought, they are replaced by Heaven and Medicine, which are both conceived of as impersonal deities. Man, the actor, uses "Medicine"; he does not worship it. Baigan's thought was more secular than Shōsan's; it was a popular code of ethics.

Shōsan had his own idea of medicine—the Buddhist sutras are medicine, he said, provided by the Great Healing King to help man. While Shōsan thought of medicine in spiritual terms, as being conveyed to a passive supplicant,

Baigan taught that we apply medicine ourselves; we are our own physician.

> A good physician applies anything that will cure the disease. He must be familiar with all medicines and use them all. Why should one cast aside a traditional medicine? A good doctor does not discard even one, nor does he depend on one alone.

Baigan makes it clear in this passage that he saw nothing wrong in drawing freely from the thought of Confucius, Mencius, Lao-tzu, and Chuang-tzu, the Buddhist scriptures, and even the Japanese classics. In his opinion, anything of use was truth. In a sense he was a total pragmatist, and for that reason, it is less important to know whose words he quotes than why he quotes them, or what he is attempting to "cure." He may ignore the context of the passage he quotes in an effort to advance his own argument, or he may not quote it with total accuracy, but this does not affect the way one understands his thinking.

Baigan treated religion and thought as methodology, but he also regarded religion as a means of disseminating ideas. Thus he saw no contradiction in following Shinto, Buddhist, and Confucianist tenets simultaneously. He likened them to gold, silver, and copper coins. His was the kind of thinking that makes it possible today for Japanese to observe the rites of passage of their children at a Shinto shrine, be married in a Christian church, and hold funerals at a Buddhist temple. Such behavior does not reflect lack of principle. Rather, it is based on a well-defined world view.

True Heart

Baigan described himself as a creature of logic, and, indeed, he was unable to grasp the interrelation of the cosmos, man, and society on the religious level of Shōsan's thought. He believed only in what he could grasp logically. Of particular interest is his exhaustive consideration of human nature. He used the term *sei* (nature), but it meant little to the average person in Baigan's time, and so one of Baigan's disciples, Teshima Toan (1718–86), substituted the word *honshin* (true heart). The term *honshin* appears in the Buddhist scriptures, and of course Shōsan used it as well. When we unconsciously speak of *honshin* today, however, it is in the sense developed by Toan.

Interestingly, all Japanese recognize the existence of *honshin*, and the language is filled with expressions that include it. "Kimi no honshin ni tōte miro" (Do you feel guilty? or lit., "Ask your heart of hearts"); "Sore wa kimi ga honshin kara itte iru no ka" (Do you really mean it?); "Honshin ni oite wa akunin wa inai" (No one is evil at heart); and "Honshin dōri ni shite ireba yoi" (Do as your heart commands). As in these expressions, *honshin* is a highly abstract idea whose existence may be impossible to prove logically, and which may defy substantive definition. It is an article of faith, and any Japanese who denies its existence will find himself out on a limb in his community.

In the section in *Shokunin nichiyō* about the artisan and his daily life, Shōsan declared that faith means, first and foremost, having faith in oneself. A person who says he has lost faith in himself loses credibility in the eyes of society; in the same way, if he were told, "Ask your heart of hearts" and he responded by disavowing the premise, saying, "Heart? What *are* you talking about?" other people would quickly lose confidence in him. The social order in Japan is based on, among other things, the "true heart" that all people are assumed to have.

It stands to reason, therefore, that a society whose basic

ideas depend on the existence of the Creator constructs theology—the study of God, whereas a society whose thought patterns assume *honshin* in everyone pursues Shingaku—the study of the Heart. How, then, was Baigan's system of popular ethics constructed? Simply put, one learned how to live in accordance with one's heart of hearts. Religion and philosophy were medicines intended to help one achieve this end; they existed for the benefit of *honshin*, not vice versa.

Honesty lay at the base of Shōsan's philosophy, as it did with Baigan's. It meant being honest with one's *honshin*. At times, this required lying to others, but Japanese find no contradiction there.

When a Japanese finds himself in a culture whose people believe in the existence of God but not in *honshin*, he discovers that his own system of ethics is as incomprehensible to those people as organized theology is in Japan. There is no mention of anything comparable to *honshin* in the Bible. In the Japanese translation of both Old and New Testaments one finds the word *honshin* only once in each, in the expression *honshin kara* (from the heart), in expressions that can be interpreted to mean "in earnest" or "with deep sincerity." *Honshin* in Japanese is sometimes used in this sense, but this is not the original meaning of the word. Nowhere in the Bible is *honshin* used in the sense of "heart of hearts."

What, then, is *honshin*? We use the word constantly, but we rarely think about its meaning. Baigan felt compelled to seek out its real meaning. He reasoned that because the admonition to reflect on one's own behavior is a command to examine one's heart of hearts, *honshin* is therefore both the motivation for introspection and the standard by which one measures one's actions. If so, an individual has both a self that causes him to reflect and a self that is caused to reflect, and the former is *honshin*, which demands self-reflection.

Then Baigan found himself deadlocked as he tried to develop this reasoning: The moment one becomes conscious of one's reflection-motivating self and wonders if this is one's *honshin*, one realizes the presence of another self, the self that is doing the wondering. Perhaps *that*, then, is the *honshin*, the self that is wondering, one thinks, and immediately another self is present. Obviously any number of selves could appear if this process were repeated, but it would not necessarily lead to understanding. Until one clearly grasps *honshin*, it is impossible to live according to one's heart, to become one with one's heart.

It was his teacher Oguri Ryōun who helped him find a way out by saying that human nature, or *honshin*, "has no eyes"; in other words, man cannot perceive his own nature in this way. Baigan then understood that the two selves, contemplating and contemplated, are one and the same, just as the individual who is looking at nature is the same as nature itself.

At this point, Baigan thought he had made a breakthrough in his predicament, but he was not yet satisfied. A creature of logic, he continued to pursue this reasoning. He asked himself whether one who is deaf, dumb, and blind also possesses *honshin*. Yes, he concluded, that person, too, has *honshin*. In this case, he thought, even an infant does. So he proceeded to observe an infant. He found that the only thing a baby does for itself is breathe, and even breathing is not an act of volition, but of compulsion. The force that compels its breathing gives the infant life, Baigan perceived, and he then posited a continuous natural order that sustains its life, regardless of volition. Because all men lived in conformity with this order, it must be the essence of human nature. Thus, to

Baigan, the infant, which personified the archetypal conformity to the natural order, was a sage, and this sage
epitomized the human *honshin*.

The Way of Nature

Going further, Baigan wondered, would all the world's
problems be solved if everyone were as honest and natural
as an infant? Would people attain happiness if they simply
pursued their occupations as Buddhist practice? Like
Shōsan, Baigan regarded everyday labor as a form of
practical asceticism. The two men's thinking differed,
however, in their respective vantage points on society.

Until the age of forty-two, Shōsan was a government
official and a former samurai. He had played a part in the
unification of the country and the establishment of the
Tokugawa shogunate. Baigan was a member of the merchant class whose working life was like that of any other
shop employee. Thus Shōsan's perspective tended to be
national, taking in the whole country, while Baigan concentrated more narrowly on the social significance of the
merchant class. His thinking was less state-oriented than
society-oriented. Baigan's point of departure—that an infant is a sage—and his attempt to grasp rationally the
relationship between the social order and the order within
a man's heart clearly reveal how different their thinking
was.

Because an infant manifested the continuous order of
the cosmos, it was a sage, but if everyone remained an
infant all their lives there could be no society at all. If
Baigan had lived aloof from the world he might have
thought differently, but he was deeply involved in the real
world, the senior clerk in a store. Just as Shōsan developed

a fundamental world view and a social ethic based on it, so did Baigan. He created a theory by which the social order could be brought into conformity with the continuous cosmic order—"goodness"—and the infant sage who embodied it. In addition to concepts he shared with Shōsan, Baigan's philosophy contained two other ideas: "form embodies Heart" and "self-restraint and order." In a sense, these are a social version of the religious element in Shōsan's thought.

The idea of "form embodies Heart" was based on the way Baigan observed living things. Animals were of course part of the natural order. What then determined their Heart? In Baigan's opinion, it was the form of the creature. In *Tohi mondō* he writes: "We are part of creation. All things are born of Heaven. Could any Heart exist apart from things? Things themselves are Heart." "The form of a thing immediately reveals its Heart. Mosquito larvae in water do not sting humans. Once they become mosquitoes, however, they sting. Form determines Heart. Fauna are totally innocent. Their behavior is consistent with their form. All follow the laws of nature. The sage knows the laws." This principle applies to human beings as well, and the basis of the social order is the human form, and by definition, the Heart.

Baigan's philosophy was developed later by Kamata Ryūō into a sort of theory resembling evolutionism, and by Fuse Shōō into a mechanistic view of the cosmos. To follow the development from Shōsan to these men is fascinating; this exercise alone proves that the Tokugawa period was definitely not the stagnant period that it is so often portrayed to be. Be that as it may, let us return to the spirit of Japanese capitalism, and consider the social ethics that developed from Baigan's "form embodies Heart" concept.

He believed that the form of a man, as of an animal, determined how he lived. While a horse was shaped to consume grass, man was created to feed himself through the fruit of his labors. By living according to its form, the horse conforms with the continuous order of the cosmos, and in so doing, contributes to the formation of animal society; in the same way, when man lives according to his form, his social order conforms with the cosmos.

Because the sage knows the laws, to follow nature is to act in accordance with the rules set by the sage. In the case of a horse, one must place a bit in its mouth to keep it orderly, but the same method will not work when dealing with a bull. It was the sages who established the precepts that accord with the form of man. And to live in accordance with one's form was to follow the order of nature.

Japanese feel comfortable when something follows a certain prescribed form. To them, this is the natural way. Like the word "*honshin*," "natural" and "unnatural" come quickly into speech, without forethought as to their meaning. The word "natural" is used often with the meaning of a natural or proper social act or phenomenon. To do something in disregard of its propriety or accepted inevitability is unnatural. At times, one's words or actions are criticized as being unnatural—what a Westerner might call "unfair." Such behavior or speech cannot be forgiven, no matter how justifiable it may be; to the Japanese sensitivity, it is beyond rationalization.

Most of us do not give a second thought as to why we speak of "natural" or "unnatural" things, comparing them with nature, just as we do not think about the meaning of *honshin*. Baigan, however, was driven to deliberate hard on that question. And as we have seen he concluded that because an animal's Heart is embodied in its form, it is a part of the natural order, and man is no exception. Thus

Heart (the inner order) and the cosmos (the natural order) are one and the same, linked together by form. Form also links the individual and society, and therefore to live according to one's form—to follow the Way—is natural. A sage was one who understood this Way.

Profit Is Just

How did Baigan derive this conception? His thought process was closely linked to the way he saw his own social class. To Suzuki Shōsan, the merchant was a sort of traveling salesman, a "pilgrim" whose journeys linked supply and demand. By Baigan's time, however, commercial business was carried on by organized groups whose purpose was to realize a profit, and as a class, these people were vigorous entrepreneurs. Indeed, it was commonly noted that, "To outward appearances this land is ruled by the samurai class, but in reality it is ruled by merchants" (see chapter 4). Yet there is no denying that, in the context of the social order of the time, their activities were considered just antisocial enough to make them distasteful, at least suspect.

In effect, Baigan sought to give a fair assessment of the role of the merchant in contemporary society by identifying his raison d'être. He believed that a Way governed all four classes, including the merchant class. He urged the people of his class to be faithful to the Way, and tried to persuade the other classes to accept the merchant on that basis. "How could the Way of the merchant differ from that of samurai, peasant, or artisan? Mencius also said that there is but one Way. Samurai, peasants, artisans, and merchants are one under Heaven. How could there be two different ways?" Baigan asked.

At the same time, he offered a clear argument in defense of the merchant. The dealings of a merchant are for the good of the world. Both the artisan and the farmer are rewarded for their labors with remuneration that is essentially the same as a samurai's stipend. Without labor, how could the people of the world carry on? The merchant is allowed his profit—that is his stipend. But people criticize him, saying that his activities are not part of the Way—that he does nothing but greedily pursue profit. They despise him and shun him. Why do they deprecate the merchant alone? If a merchant sold things at cost, realizing no profit, this would violate the law of the land. Baigan would not deny the merchant his profit. Profit was just, but like the reward earned by the samurai, only if it were gained through faithful and earnest effort.

> My "stipend" is the profits I earn through transactions. I receive them from my customers. If they tell me to come, I will come, just as a samurai will hasten to fulfill his duty. Greediness is not in question. It is hard for a samurai to follow the Way of the Warrior if he cannot receive any stipend from his master. To claim that his wish for a stipend is against the Way is to say that Confucius, Mencius, and the other great sages did not know the Way.

Baigan pursued this line of thought by asking how the merchant could follow the Way without falling prey to greed. Interestingly, his answer is to pursue practical rationality in business. First, he said, just as a samurai who receives a stipend from his lord but does not serve him faithfully cannot be called a true samurai, a merchant who is insincere with his customers is no merchant. Most important is sincerity toward the consumer. And, "Above all, be frugal. If you needed one *kanme* [960 *mon* = value by weight] until now, make do with only 700 *mon*. If you gain one *kanme* of profit, reduce it to 900 *mon.*" He advises merchants to cut costs by 30 percent and reduce their profits by 10 percent. Furthermore, one should "keep detailed accounts and always exercise restraint." At all times one must strive to serve one's customers and never succumb to greed. To become avaricious is to depart from the Way and go into certain bankruptcy. On the other hand, when one seeks always to serve, one is sure to prosper.

Of greatest importance here is the concept of frugality. Baigan calls it the most vital factor in practicing the Way. He also makes a clear distinction between frugality and stinginess—greed. Baigan's frequent admonitions on frugality are best represented in his last book, *Ken'yaku seika ron* (Thrift: the proper way to manage a household). It is indeed instructive to read the works of Baigan, Shōsan, and others, for they expound on the virtues that foster attitudes and patterns of behavior conducive to saving and the accumulation of capital. If the people see a religious significance in everyday labor and make other considerations secondary in their work, and if at the same time they believe that the pursuit of practical rationality is proper and find spiritual satisfaction in so behaving, they are well equipped to become successful capitalists. When people think and act this way, it is not surprising that their profits should grow naturally, outstripping others.

Frugality as Virtue

Japanese firmly believe that waste and extravagance are sinful, though profit is not. A powerful politician* who

---

*The author is referring to former prime minister Tanaka Kakuei.

keeps decorative carp worth several thousand dollars apiece in his garden naturally draws criticism. It is not contradictory, therefore, that a leading business executive* is trusted by society if he leads a frugal existence. His income may be high, but if he demonstrates self-control by limiting his personal expenditures, he is highly respected. Baigan's frugality is based on a premise of self-control, and at the same time it underlies order in "the house," by which he meant family enterprise. In other words, the idea of curbing one's greedy desire for profit and channeling all one's efforts into serving the consumer implies self-control vis-à-vis the outside world, but this channeling of energy invariably leads one to seek rationalization also, which means the pursuit of inner self-control, or thrift. Thrift is a consumer logic, which we find nowhere in the writings of Shōsan. No doubt one reason for this lack is that Shōsan was a Zen monk, in addition to the fact that the level of consumption in his time was so low that there was no need to preach frugality. One result is that he never tried to set down rules governing consumption in terms of Buddhist practice.

Baigan, however, lived after the prosperity of the Genroku era (1688–1704) ended, and he was keenly interested in the matter of consumption. Why on earth must human beings consume, he pondered. Again, to find out, he felt compelled to return to the most elementary level, and spent considerable effort in answering detractors in the most basic terms. His doctrine of frugality seems to have been widely criticized. First, it was said that frugality amounted to stinginess, which was motivated by greed. One critic wrote, for example: "When a saint rules over people, he does so like parents raising their children. Wife, children, and servants are subjects under the head of a

---

*Dokō Toshiwo, now honorary president of the Japan Federation of Economic Organizations (*Keidanren*).

family. It is the duty of the head of the house to rule his subjects peacefully. Man's joy consists first of all in clothing, food, and shelter." To deprive them of this basic enjoyment, he told Baigan, was wrong because "it derives from greed."

Baigan replied, "You have said that clothing, food, and shelter are the joy of man . . . but these three items are what man cannot do without. He enjoys living in peace by keeping himself from hunger and cold. The *Chou-li* (Rites of Chou) states that even if a dwelling is not splendid, it is adequate as long as it does not leak; even if clothes are not made of silk, they are sufficient if they provide warmth; and even if food and drink are not fine delicacies, if they fill the stomach, they are adequate. According to the Discourses of Confucius, a sage will neither eat greedily nor live in a luxurious house." This idea bears an interesting resemblance to the Puritan ethical code, that one should wear no more than is truly necessary.

Baigan's thinking on this was definitely influenced by the times in which he lived. He wrote: "Look at the society around you and you will notice that nothing declines so easily as merchants. The root cause is an illness called stupidity. Stupidity turns quickly into vanity. Stupidity and vanity are two different things, but they always go together." Baigan noted, as an example, that tradesmen, imitating the samurai, had their employees address the mistress of the house as "oku" and made lavish pilgrimages to shrines. This kind of vanity is enough to bankrupt a man before he knows it, he said. The whereabouts of some well-known and wealthy merchants of Kyoto and Osaka who were listed in the official register thirty or forty years ago is no longer known. Many have been reduced to such poverty that they cannot even hire a servant. All this comes about through stupidity and vanity, said Baigan; to develop a resistance to those diseases, it is necessary to understand the basic question of why man consumes.

More important, the "diseases" can upset the functioning order of a life. Baigan cites the experience of witnessing a fire in Osaka. Describing the fire, he uses it to illustrate human behavior when public order is undermined. The damage will not be irreparable in a time of peace, but in a period of civil war, Baigan warns, law and order has deteriorated so that a person who flees a fire leaving all his possessions behind may even be stripped of his clothing by highwaymen.

> Can one be choosy about food and clothing during a war? There is nothing to wear but lice-filled clothes. One cannot complain that cotton clothes are heavy. One should wear them with reverent gratitude. Food is scarce, and most people are hungry. Can one complain that one does not like boiled barley or rice gruel? If someone gives you something to eat, you should regard that person as a god or a Buddha. Is it not a blessing that now in this reign all people throughout the land are being fed?

In response to these remarks, Baigan is challenged again. The stories about tradesmen are indeed interesting, says the critic, but they do not illuminate great moral principles applicable to the whole of society, including samurai and court nobles. To this logical observation, Baigan replies, "You say that the principles that concern tradesmen are trivial and not widely applied. I do not think so. A principle is the same, regardless of what job or duty you are engaged in." Thus Baigan regards the class distinctions among warriors, farmers, artisans, and tradesmen as based essentially on differences in duties and occupations, and he thinks they are governed by the same moral principles.

This idea runs through Baigan's entire discussion. He

repeatedly emphasizes that the ethic he proposes is not limited to merchants. He says:

> If frugality is practiced with conviction, the household—and the nation—will be in good order. Peace will reign throughout the land. Is this not the most fundamental ethic? Frugality is, after all, a means of moral training that helps people put their houses in order. According to the Confucian treatise *Ta-hsüeh* (The great learning), the most important concern for everyone, from emperor on down to commoner, is to attend to his moral cultivation. In moral training, should it matter whether one is warrior, farmer, artisan, or merchant? What is the subject of moral training? It is none other than the Heart.

Thus, the pursuit of "economy" and "rationality" in Baigan's terms can be incorporated into ethics, no matter what class one belongs to. What is required is self-control, which Baigan believes is the basis of the social order.

Such thinking is still with us. Japanese resist the idea of allowing themselves to be controlled by external strictures, such as laws and company rules and regulations; they try to maintain order by inner self-control. If this is the basis of our society, then it is not surprising that Baigan's thinking should be taken for granted in Japan; that keeping very expensive carp should be criticized, and the frugal life of a businessman praised.

Why Is "Whistle Blowing" Bad?

According to Baigan, acts that deny the principle of frugality are derived from "desire for fame," "greed for gain," or "carnal appetite." To be miserly in order to accumulate wealth is not frugality. It is greed for gain, he says. And just as miserliness arises out of greed for gold and silver, so wasteful consumption comes from greed for show, a desire to gain fame even if it may cost a fortune. Carnal appetite is another kind of greed.

Frugality has nothing to do with such greed. "Because I have grasped a principle applicable to all classes of people, even though their occupations differ, the way of the samurai that I teach applies likewise to the farmer, artisan, and merchant. The reverse is also true. Why should I teach frugality to the four classes separately?" says Baigan. "I emphasize frugality simply because with it, everyone can go back to the honesty he or she had at birth." A baby is sacred; to be as a baby is honesty, and this honesty is in conformity with the continuous order of the universe. Frugality, Baigan taught, is a way to return to this state.

If Shōsan had lived to see the consumer culture of the Genroku era, he also would undoubtedly have discussed consumption as Buddhist practice. Baigan affirms this view:

> Because people originally come from Heaven, everyone is a child of Heaven. He is a microcosm of heaven, and therefore he should have no selfish desire. He should know what belongs to him and what belongs to others. He should receive back what he lent out, and return what he borrowed. He should never be self-centered, but do only what he is naturally intended to do. This is honesty. If all people practice this honesty, all members of society will be in harmony and all peoples from around the seven seas will be brothers. This is my ultimate goal.

Thus Baigan emphasizes that man originally is free from greed, as is Heaven; that honesty is the way to return to this original self and once more become a heavenly microcosm. If everyone did this, order would prevail rooted in peace and harmony.

Baigan's view sounds rosy indeed, but the crux is his

concept of "honesty." Earlier we saw that to Baigan honesty meant "honesty in one's heart-of-hearts," and that it is possible to be honest even when one lies to others.

Man should be faithful to the heart, said Baigan. "What I mean by honesty is to follow the dictates of your compassion. . . . Compassion as taught by revered sages is the true Heart, and it cannot be acquired by thinking or studying. It is a natural gift under the rule of Heaven."

This idea, too, is more or less part of contemporary Japanese ethics. Japanese often refer to *jitsujō* (true heart, true emotion) when they appeal in self-defense, saying "Please understand my true emotions." They are *not* saying, "Please appreciate the facts, the actual conditions," as it is often interpreted to mean. Within a pseudo-consanguineous society, this idea becomes a communal ethic. Peace and harmony first and foremost are principles of the community, and "reflex compassion" stemming from the true heart is highly esteemed. And to follow this compassion is regarded as honesty.

One who discloses to outsiders a scandal within one's community is a "repulsive villain," and this applies to every organization in Japan, from the Marubeni Corporation—witness the case of the Lockheed payoffs—to the Japan Communist party. Those who attack someone for lying for the sake of one's organization would do the same in that person's position. If someone testified before the public that his organization committed an illegal act, no one would be surprised if he were attacked for treachery and betrayal within his community and ostracized. In the face of adverse circumstances, this ethic works to build even stronger communal solidarity, and there is no doubt that it increases the organization's efficiency as a functional group. Even from this brief description of some of Baigan's central ideas, one can see how closely they match the social structure of Japan today.

International Version of Baigan's Thought

Baigan did more than preach; he practiced his ideas in actual life. He died on September 24, 1744, soon after *Ken'yaku seika ron* was published, and according to records, not a single item that seemed superfluous or unnecessary was found among his belongings. All that remained at his home after his death were three chests of books, a bookrest, desk, inkstone, drafts of the answers to questions he was most often asked, and clothes and utensils for daily use. His life can be described as the simple, clean, and untroubled life of an ordinary salaried worker. And as is usually true of salaried workers, Baigan, too, tried to avoid drawing attention to himself.

After his death, however, because of the efforts his disciples made to spread and explain his philosophy, Baigan and his teaching became famous. Teshima Toan did more than most others to promote and publicize the Ishida school of popular ethics (Sekimon Shingaku). It was Toan, we should recall, who had rephrased Baigan's term *sei* (human nature), calling it *honshin* (heart of hearts), so that people might better understand it. Toan also gave the name *hatsumei* (discovery) to a sort of religious conversion that one could attain by following the popular ethics set forth by Ishida Baigan.

At first, Baigan's teachings were popular chiefly in the Kansai area, but after 1779, when the academy called Sanzensha was established by Nakazawa Dōni (1725–1803) in Nihonbashi, they rapidly attracted a large, devoted following in Edo. As many as twenty-one new academies were set up by disciples of Dōni to teach Baigan's popular ethics. Dōni travelled in over twenty-seven provinces, covering almost the entire country except Kyushu, to promote Baigan's philosophy.

By about this time, the Ishida system of ethics was being widely accepted by samurai as well as townspeople. But Baigan had always considered his views universal, applicable to all the classes of society. Their growing popularity might also have been spurred by the groping attempts by the samurai class for something resembling a "merchant rationality." Later, some of the ruling elite, including Kyoto Deputy Matsudaira Izunokami and Osaka City Commissioner Kuze Isenokami, began attending lectures on Ishida ethics. Many of the individual *han* (domain) governments also made a point of inviting lecturers from the Ishida school to instruct the people of their domains.

In the meantime, Baigan's popular ethics itself underwent little evolution. Although disciples like Fuse Shōō and Kamata Ryūō were influential in bringing some minor new developments, as a whole the philosophy remained very close to what Baigan had propounded. One concept that did not come into his theoretical purview was the question of political responsibility.

By this time, merchants had become so powerful that they were actually the strongest class, as they controlled the economy throughout Japan. But political responsibility was still the exclusive sphere of the samurai class. Baigan took it for granted that as long as the samurai kept order in society, merchants should tolerate their ranking above the other three social classes. Clearly "peace favors the merchant." Baigan was totally opposed to war or conflict. But he believed it the samurai's duty and responsibility—not his own or that of any other nonsamurai—to prevent war. If the warriors maintained the peace, tradesmen could concentrate fully on their businesses. This attitude contrasts sharply with European merchants, who at one point mobilized themselves to form a council to take charge of urban politics. Baigan's ideas could never have generated such a movement, much less given birth to a bourgeois revolution.

In the intellectual and social history of the Edo period, no strong ideas aimed at changing the establishment ever came out of the merchant class. Revolutionary or semirevolutionary thinking was familiar to Suzuki Shōsan and others who lived at the time when one system had collapsed and a new one was in the process of formation. As the new system took more permanent shape, one's daily labors were seen as having religious significance. The teachings of Shōsan and others encouraged people to find fulfillment in doing their routine duties. At the same time, a rational act done in the context of a functional group was turned into a service to a communal group. Increasingly people poured their "religious" enthusiasm into their daily work, which cemented the new social pattern ever more tightly.

In seeking the best way to work and live, Baigan's thinking was based on a fixed social order. The logical extension of such thinking would be an ever more rigid, unmovable society. It was natural that when merchants as a functional group became a communal group, their minds should lean toward ideas like the basically conservative philosophy of the Ishida school of popular ethics. This is one reason why Baigan's thought was so widely embraced.

Japanese leaders today in their dealings with other countries think like Baigan did, and they are given strong support from the people in this regard. The earth has shrunk—its parts are in close contact, as Japan's were in the days of her isolation from the outside world. Stability and order in the world is what today's Japanese "merchants" most desire in order to secure overseas markets. But they are reluctant to share the responsibility for keeping world order. They want the United States or the United Nations to do the job. Indeed, Baigan's thinking now has an international version.

7

THE CAPITALIST LOGIC
OF THE SAMURAI

A set of ideas forced on the people soon fades. But one born from among the populace will not die. It is so deeply rooted in the social fabric that it will survive and possibly flourish no matter what shifts in power take place. Eventually it may even have an effect on the leadership.

The Sekimon Shingaku (Ishida school of popular ethics), which I described in the previous chapter, is often identified with the Establishment, but anyone who dismisses it as such—just another ruling class ideology—has probably not carefully read the works of Baigan, founder of the Ishida school. Clearly his ideas were not derived from the ruling elite. Baigan was from the lowest of the four Edo period classes: samurai, farmer, artisan, and merchant. And, as a member of the merchant class, he was no more than a humble senior clerk (*bantō*) in a small commercial enterprise. His career as a merchant was ordinary, with no distinguishing achievements, and not particularly successful; had he not been moved by some unaccountable sense of mission to open a private school, and had it not flourished, he would have lived and died an anonymous clerk, passing unknown into history.

Baigan's whole existence was rooted in the masses. The

basis of his approach was popular thought, what he culled from his immediate surroundings. What he learned, he learned from "that most colossal of scriptures—society." Because of his roots and self-education he did not have the perverted vanity of some intellectuals who insist that theirs is popular thought, that they are with the people. Actually, the very claim that "I am with the people" implies that "I am not part of them." Baigan's life and thought were so unquestionably part of the people that it was never necessary to say so. With no formal schooling, he turned to the ancient sages—and his own observations—for the foundations of his thinking.

How was it that a mere clerk could come up with a system of thought with such broad appeal. What Baigan developed was no less than a capitalist ethic, but for a simple clerk to do this and to build it into a highly influential philosophy required certain preconditions: There had to be some logic of capital present in the society from the outset. Where there is no logic of capital, no capitalist ethic can take root. Yet the term "logic of capital," even though it represents an important social orientation and appeared frequently in the Japanese press for a time after World War II, has not always been understood clearly. The peculiar phrase "citizens' logic versus capitalist logic," for example, enjoyed a postwar vogue, but it was highly unlikely that anyone at the time could have explained exactly what the logic of capital meant.

Any logical system is founded on a truism that stands firm, like a numerical formula. The truism at the base of the logic of capital is, most simply, that profits accrue only when there is capital. Unless this is established as common knowledge in the society, the logic of capital will not survive there. The modern term "capital" (*shihon*) did not exist in the Tokugawa period, but the concept was quite adequately represented by a more appropriate phrase, *kane oya* (money parent). Ihara Saikaku (1642–93), Tokugawa period novelist, admonished in *Yorozu no fumi hōgu* (Scraps of letters of every kind): "It is quite difficult to succeed in business these days without the backing of a *kane oya*. It is too bad that people do not realize this." Substitute "bank" for "money parent," and you have a statement made three hundred years ago that is still valid. Will borrowing from a money parent assure your future? By no means. Saikaku warns that "the two most fearful things in the world are drunkenness and interest on borrowed money." To avoid the latter, he says, one must have his own money, or capital, even if the amount is small. This is the Way of the Townsman.

A character in the play *Nebiki no kadomatsu* (The uprooted pine) (1718) by Chikamatsu Monzaemon (1653–1724) declares: "The samurai seeks fame and sacrifices profit, but the townsman dismisses fame and makes profit. He amasses gold and silver. This is what he calls his Way." "To exalt until death gold and silver as one would the gods and Buddhas until death; this is the Way of Heaven for the townsman."

Saikaku, however, went further by asserting that the same principle applies not only to urban merchants but to everyone, even Buddhist monks and Shintō priests. In other words, basic to the logic of capital is a truth self-evident to everyone. The most important activity in your life regardless of whether you are a samurai, farmer, artisan, merchant, Buddhist monk, Shintō priest, or anything else, is always to follow the God of Thrift and save money. Next to your real parents, this is the "parent of your destiny," writes Saikaku. Thus, in Saikaku's view, two absolute necessities in life are one's "parent of destiny," or personal capital, and the "money parent" that

117

finances one. Trying to convince people that only capital will bring profit, he urged, "In this world one cannot make a profit without money."

Secret of Japan's Miracle

The idea that only capital can create profit crops up frequently in the essays and fiction of the Genroku era. As a principle, it produced two fundamentally different reactions in the Edo period. One was the simplistic assumption, often made by journalists today, that the logic of capital was antithetical to the logic of the samurai and was evil in itself. Such critics disparaged anyone who pursued profit and rejected the type of personality that was attracted to the logic of capital. The other reaction was acceptance of the principle as natural and eagerness to apply it for the benefit of society as a whole. This attitude led to the attempt to establish an ethic appropriate to the logic of the townspeople.

Baigan was wholeheartedly committed to the latter approach. Indeed, it may have been an inevitable consequence of the Genroku era, when the logic of capital flourished, that someone should contemplate the ethic of capitalism and develop it as Baigan did. And coming from the merchant class was definitely an advantage, for the samurai class tended to be antagonistic to the logic of capital. Some samurai, however, accepted the axiom that only capital can product profit, and that profit was often necessary. They recognized the logic of capital and tried to apply it in government. This was possible because certain preconditions were already present that paved the way for samurai acceptance of the logic of capital.

There is no nation today that has no capitalistic elements

at all in its economy and government. If there are differences, it is because some operate on state capitalism, others on monarchic, social, or private capitalism. It is hardly anomalous, then, that in Japan of the Edo period a strong strain of *han* (feudal domain) capitalism existed in which domain enterprises functioned according to the logic of capital and followed that logic in local government. This was the idea of "Han, Inc.," as it were, which emphasized "enriching the *han*." In my belief, it provided the prototype for the Meiji policy of "enriching the nation (*fukoku*)," and for "Japan, Inc." after World War II. Also not surprising, it was the samurai more than the merchants who had to undergo the painful groping for a workable system.

It is said that Japan is a society of imitators who cannot create anything original by experimentation, and trial and error, but the samurai class throughout the Edo period did just that and came up with hard-won, solid results all their own. Japan's success in the Meiji period was brought about by making best use of the achievements of this long painstaking endeavor by samurai—and incorporating the popular ethic discussed in the previous chapter. Human endeavor contains no miracles. Something that looks like a miracle simply reflects the observer's ignorance. A magic show delights the audience with its surprises, but the magician, who knows the tricks, counts on certain results. If the magician were to get some unexpected results, this might be called a miracle, but the successful efforts made in the Meiji period and after World War II were thoroughly planned. They are not miracles, but the natural outcome of well-thought-out activities.

The Genroku era was a time of gaiety and extravagance among the townspeople. To some, their carryings-on represented a kind of resistance to the strict ethic of the samurai. There were other wealthy townsmen who tried to imitate the samurai way of life. One such group, called the "Rain Dragon Society," were particularly fervid imitators of the samurai way. Conversely, some samurai imitated townsmen. Ōno Kurobei, a retainer of the Akō domain who appears in "The Forty-seven Rōnin" as a profit-seeker, is a typical example. It was this type of samurai, often described as *shibō shōkon* (samurai in appearance, merchant in spirit), who actually managed the feudal domains in the Tokugawa period.

In the Kyōhō era (1716–35), whether one was qualified to take charge of clan administration or not depended solely on one's ability to do the job. Birth, proven loyalty, or skill in the martial arts were secondary. Most important was whether one could fully exploit the logic of capital and its underlying principle. The logic of the samurai was impotent. "Orthodox" samurai who continued to live by the samurai logic were nettled, but they were no longer useful to society. "Today's world is for those skilled at ciphers. No one needs those who practice the orthodoxy of chivalry." "It is an out-of-date samurai who puts honor ahead of profit; that is no longer fashionable." Nevertheless, seeing that they could not adjust to the new priority on merit and practical skills, and finding themselves bypassed as useless, in effect, they tried all the harder to impress their own raison d'être on others, brandishing the outdated authority of prescribed rank. They despised the "renegade" samurai-turned-entrepreneur for discarding the time-honored spirit of their class—the values that compelled a warrior to run before his horse in battle and force his way into the thick of the enemy to decapitate the foe or perform glorious deeds, risking his life for his lord. Society no longer needed that kind of samurai.

Rising Capitalists, Declining Samurai

The third-generation head of the Mitsui family financial group, Takafusa, is famous as the author of *Chōnin kōken-roku* (Precautionary notes for the townsman), written in the early eighteenth century to record and pass on the rules governing the family business. He cautions his successors by citing more than forty examples of once-wealthy merchant families in Kyoto who had gone bankrupt. "The samurai employs whatever strategem he needs in order to win. That is what he would do in a battle," says Takafusa. Because the samurai and the merchant differ in their thinking, if the latter is careless enough to lend money to the former, he may be unable to collect the money and go bankrupt. Actually, many wealthy entrepreneurs were ruined that way. Takafusa uses the phrase "wicked prestigious families" to describe notorious upper-class borrowers who failed to repay debts. But capital flows only to safe places, and eventually the refusal to honor debts worked against the samurai as a whole. Now the samurai had to humble himself before the merchant in order to borrow money. As the Confucian scholar Dazai Shundai (1680–1747) put it, all the warrior class "rely on merchants to conduct both public and private affairs. Even high-ranking officials fear and respect the merchants to a considerable degree."

No matter how hard the samurai tried to stress the logic of the warrior and assume authority, they had no place in an age without war. Like it or not, those warriors who could not become economic bureaucrats had to admit defeat. The Edo period samurai had to follow the logic of capital and become managers in "Han, Inc.," or become economic bureaucrats. In that sense, some samurai did turn into merchants.

There was a very strict rule in this transformation, however: In applying the logic of capital, aware that capital alone would bring profit, they had to remember always that they were doing so for the sake of their clan, never for personal gain. This rule is akin to the thinking of Suzuki Shōsan, Ishida Baigan, and others who preached against avarice and taught that everything a person did was ascetic practice. It became one of the basic rules in all domain policies. In other words, the domain as a functional group was run in accordance with the logic of capital, but the ultimate goal was the continued existence of the domain as a communal group. Whether domain or company, this rule applies as long as the organization is both a functional and a communal group.

Many elements combined to create internal strife within the domains during the Tokugawa period, but they can be roughly divided into two categories. One was the confrontation between the townsman-type samurai-turned-merchant who followed the logic of capital and the advocates of the conservative samurai logic who felt compelled to show their loyalty by being always ready to rush headlong into battle. The other type was between two groups that both accepted the logic of capital. One consisted of those who made personal gain, the other of those who did not. The former included some of low birth who rose to important positions in domain administration. Men less talented had to take insignificant posts, even if they were of good lineage. Thus, the two groups clashed.

Several daimyo became famous and are revered even today as enlightened lords. The management of their retainers was superior in every way. Following the logic of capital, they themselves lived frugally and encouraged the martial arts so that those who could not participate in domain management might find a satisfactory raison d'être and psychological satisfaction in such activities. Let us take a look at the management methods and achievements of a typical enlightened lord.

Yōzan's Radical Cutback

Among the best-known "wise" daimyo during the Tokugawa period were Uesugi Yōzan of the Yonezawa domain, Mōri Shigenari (Chōshū), Hosokawa Shigekata (Higo), and Tokugawa Harusada (Kishū). Of the four, Uesugi Yōzan had the most difficult circumstances to deal with in carrying out reform plans, but his is an informative case study. First, having been adopted into the Uesugi family from a small clan, he was literally a stranger to the domain. At one point, seven conservative senior retainers attempted to oust Yōzan, and in their impeachment note, they argued that he was "not in the direct lineage of the Uesugi house; he came from another family." They deeply resented him, an intruder, even though to give voice to such an attitude was unthinkably insolent in an era of strict feudal mores when each person was expected to keep his place and keep it punctiliously. Yōzan faced opposition so bitter that even these rules were broken.

There were other difficulties. The Uesugi family had been one of the most powerful in Japan under the headship of Kenshin (1530–78). The family possessed domains yielding 3,000,000 *koku* (1 *koku* = about 5 American bushels) of rice, as well as gold mines on Sado Island. After the death of Kenshin, his adopted son Kagekatsu succeeded as the second head of the family, but internal strife and external pressure forced the Uesugi to move to Aizu, where they controlled a domain producing 1,200,000 *koku*. When the Battle of Sekigahara was joined in 1600, Kagekatsu took the side of the anti-Tokugawa forces, who lost. The family was compelled to move from Aizu to Yonezawa, a poor 300,000 *koku* domain. The fourth to succeed as family head, Tsunakatsu, did not produce an heir, and the bakufu nearly forced the family line to die out. Only because of its former prestige was the Uesugi family allowed to continue by means of adopting Tsunanori, a son of Kira Kōzukenosuke. When Tsunanori became the fifth head of the Uesugi family, the domain was reduced to 150,000 *koku*.

This saga can be compared to the decline of a company that starts with ¥30 billion capital and, because of business failure, watches that capital erode after continuous mismanagement and other failures, first to 12 billion, and eventually to 1.5 billion. It ends up worth one-twentieth its original value. But, while a modern company can cut the number of employees in proportion to capital reduction, a feudal clan could not. Financial problems alone made management of the Yonezawa domain exceedingly difficult, but added to this, when Tsunanori succeeded as the fifth lord of Yonezawa, the head of the clan was not even a blood relative of the Uesugi. Generations later, Yōzan (also called Harunori) was also adopted; he was the second son of Akizuki Taneyoshi, lord of Takanabe in the province of Hyūga, Kyūshū.

In effect, then, at certain times the president of Uesugi & Co. was a Mr. Kira or Mr. Akizuki. They were recruited as president from outside the company so as to ensure its survival. To the senior retainers—top management—who were proud of their own families' continued service to the Uesugi since the time of Kenshin, these outsiders had been adopted into the family merely for the sake of expedience. It was against this background that the senior retainers finally exploded in resentment and broke some feudal taboos on behavior when Yōzan was made family head.

No stopgap measures could prevent the domain from going bankrupt. Only drastic reform would save it. Its "capital" had been reduced to one-twentieth, but the number of "employees" remained the same. Worse, these numerous employees were samurai; they were nonproducers. There were only two alternatives: either to make the samurai into a productive work force to set the domain firmly in business as a profitable enterprise, or let the clan collapse. And a commitment to the former, to survival, left no choice but to follow the logic of capital. In such a situation, the best way to proceed is obvious in retrospect, but it is by no means clear to those directly involved at the time. Yet this is not surprising, for facts do not move people as do illusions. It is the same today. We know what we must do today to solve the problems we know will occur a hundred or even fifty years from now, but even after years of discussion, people are still arguing.

What is going on in the Japan National Railways (JNR) is a good example. The JNR's share of all railway transport services is less than 14 percent today, but the attitudes of the company and its employees remain the same as when the present-day Ministry of Transport was called the Ministry of Railways (1920–43) and its share was almost 100 percent. Like the JNR's National Railways Workers' Union, Yonezawa's senior retainers were very influential in the domain. If the people in Yōzan's day rose united against their lord they could easily oust the seventeen-year-old "president" brought in from a small unrelated "company."

If the situation in the Yonezawa domain of two centuries past seems bizarre, we need only consider what later generations will probably think about the quirks of today's

Japan. In no way can we just dismiss what Yōzan's senior retainers did as mere folly.

Internal Psychological Change

Not wanting to face reality, a person or group often acts contrary to their best interests. This tendency was evident in the Yonezawa clan when Tsunanori, one of the Kira family, was adopted to become head. Although, or rather because, the domain's rice yield had fallen to 150,000 *koku*, and because Tsunanori was all too conscious of his lack of Uesugi blood, he acted all the more arrogantly, making much of ceremonial formality and old conventions. As a result, the clan spent more than it did when its total yield was 300,000 *koku*. This went on for about a century. By the time Yōzan was adopted into the Uesugi family, the economic situation had become almost hopeless.

Under such conditions, it is usually those who are not samurai who suffer most in the domain. They are heavily taxed, which weakens their willingness to work, and as production declines, their taxes grow even heavier. Then they lose all incentive even to try. Domain morale plummets and gambling becomes widespread. The fields grow barren and weed-choked, and the peasants begin to drift off into other domains. Any community whose economy weakens to this point is bound to collapse.

If collapse can be prevented at all, the first step is to make everyone involved aware of the full realities of the situation. Yōzan was only seventeen when he became lord of Yonezawa, responsible for overall management of the clan. Before proceeding, he disclosed the details of his plan for recovery to Irobe Terunaga, chief retainer on duty in Edo, to gain his endorsement. Then, along with Irobe,

Yōzan formed a lord-retainer alliance and placed their written oath in a shrine. He then carefully explained the realities of the clan's plight to all the Yonezawa retainers who were on duty in the capital. His story began: "The Uesugi are now a small family. Yet all of us, higher and lower ranks alike, still yearn to have everything running the way it used to when the Uesugi domain was large and prosperous. The Uesugi are a prestigious family, which compels them to keep up their extravagant expenditures." Yōzan then elucidated the clan's financial difficulties, concluding that, "Nothing would be less filial than to sit back and wait until the family were ruined and everyone in the domain suffered." Rather than waiting for the collapse of the family, he said, both lord and retainers should do everything they could until their last resources were exhausted. And first, above all else, they must launch a rigid program of strict frugality, he declared.

He was not so optimistic as to think that strict frugality alone would solve all their problems. He knew that as long as expenditures continued to heavily outweigh income, it would be hard to obtain loans from "money parents," hence there would be great difficulty in obtaining development funds. Thus, only a drastic reduction in expenditures would enable them to get the needed backing. In carrying out his frugality program, Yōzan never ordered his retainers to take specific actions, but rather talked extensively with them to encourage a consensus. He himself took the initiative to be frugal, so that the others would follow his example. He cut his annual salary to about one-seventh its set level, from 1,500 to 209 *ryō*, and reduced his retinue of waiting maids from more than fifty to nine.

The domain's chief executive, Chisaka Takaatsu, was summoned from Yonezawa to Edo. Yōzan tried to persuade him to do what had to be done to regain solvency. He told Chisaka that after returning to Yonezawa he intended to assemble all the domain retainers in the castle and make clear to them the gravity of the financial crisis facing the clan. He wanted to explain to them his policy of gaining and acting on a strong consensus in Yonezawa, as he had done with his retainers in Edo.

Yōzan met with opposition even at that early stage. Takaatsu replied that Yōzan's request had no precedent, and that the lord should issue a written directive to all the leading retainers in Yonezawa instead of addressing all the retainers. Yōzan compromised. He wrote out a statement of his intentions that Takaatsu could show to the retainers in Yonezawa. Whether or not he felt compelled to write the statement against his better judgment, it is fortunate for us that he did, for it is this document, which still exists, that tells us today exactly what Yōzan's policies were.

Yōzan was very aware that his course of action would be hard on everyone for a time. If they did nothing and continued as they were, the hardship might be postponed until the last moment of bankruptcy, but he believed they could avoid that. He urged his senior retainers to "practice strict frugality. Even if the people must suffer under it, I believe it is clear that this policy will eventually bring them happiness." He cited the case of Matsudaira Nobutsuna (1596–1662) who once melted down a big bronze Buddha to mint coins. Such an act would please the heart of the Buddha, wrote Yōzan. He then recalled Kenshin, illustrious leader of the Uesugi clan. Only if they did everything in their power to restore the clan, he said, would they be worthy to be considered descendants of the wise and heroic forebear. Then, even if they failed and the clan collapsed into ruin, they could find some joy in their grief.

If the clan's income was too low, the only way to compensate even part of the gap was to cut expenditures. Yōzan added that his deepest wish was for everyone to be united in the rehabilitation of the clan.

This was less an order than a solicitation; there was probably no other alternative for the seventeen-year-old adopted lord. But we should also give him credit for perceiving clearly that a complete change in attitude, an internal psychological reorientation, was necessary for everyone. Otherwise, Yōzan saw that effective reform would be hopeless, and in this he had grasped something fundamental about any community confronting deep crisis, and understood what was required for resolution of its difficulties.

Acting on the Obvious

The senior retainers rejected Yōzan's request, despite its urgency, complaining that such an important matter should not have been decided without consulting them. He had spoken directly with the retainers in Edo, they pouted, but to those in Yonezawa he merely sent a directive that was conveyed by a clan executive. Such an action was tantamount to ignoring them, they claimed, and demanded that Yōzan come to Yonezawa and talk directly with them, or they would not even consider his proposals. It became a matter of face. Yōzan wrote a letter to them this time in his own handwriting. Humbling himself more than would be expected of a feudal lord, Yōzan admitted that he had lacked consideration. "But it is no use my regretting a mistake of the past," he wrote, and asked them to please support him by carrying out his plans.

They turned down his request. In effect, they had given a vote of nonconfidence in their lord.

This brought the clan to the verge of internal strife. To prevent it, Shigesada, the former lord and Yōzan's adoptive father, intervened. He feared that if a proclamation issued in Edo by the lord of Yonezawa were rejected at home, it would mean dire trouble for the clan. Shigesada went to the castle himself and delivered a speech on behalf of the young lord. Most of the opposing retainers were there, except for Imokawa Masanori, a magistrate, who refused to attend. Most of those present were unwilling to follow their lord's requests. They assumed that because Yōzan came from a small domain, he did not know the established formalities of a large clan, and they refused to believe that the seventeen-year-old Yōzan could have conceived such a plan. Convinced that his aides must have planted such ideas in his mind, they launched a campaign to expel them.

Among the senior retainers only one, Takemata Masatsuna, supported him. Takemata could make no move, however, because a conservative group led by Imokawa kept close watch on him. Yōzan's close associates, who had been at his service, were forced to resign. The only man he could consult was his personal physician, Warashina Teisuke. Yōzan was in an extremely difficult position. Interestingly enough, while Yōzan's remaining chief advisor was a physician, the conservative faction's chief advisor also was a doctor with the same surname, Warashina Rittaku. Both were intellectuals, each being a doctor and Confucianist. Those willing to help Yōzan were either disciples of Teisuke or their friends. Takemata Masatsuna was one. With his small backing and only Teisuke to turn to for advice, Yōzan could do little, no matter what he might plan.

To compound his troubles, the Tokugawa bakufu had ordered the Yonezawa clan to "help" in building a residential mansion for the heir to the shogun west of the donjon of Edo Castle. This kind of order—to provide extremely costly "help" to the bakufu—was always dreaded by the Tokugawa period daimyo, and for the Yonezawa clan, the timing could not have been worse. It was already facing a financial crisis of its own. Yōzan sent another letter in his own handwriting to his retainers in Yonezawa, telling them the details of the clan's plight. He announced that an additional tax would be collected.

Yōzan left Edo and went back to Yonezawa. Awaiting his return was another eruption of factional strife that had been going on for generations between the *Umamawari-gumi* ("Mounted Guard") and the *Gojukki-gumi* ("Fifty Horsemen Corps"), the positions in both being hereditary. The former consisted of men whose ancestors had served the Uesugi family for generations, while the latter were descendants of those who had distinguished themselves in military service to the Nagao family, from which Uesugi Kenshin was adopted. The two groups could not seem to reconcile their rivalry even when their clan was on the verge of ruin. It was like the factional strife that continues to rend a company even when it is heading toward bankruptcy. Yōzan was modest in his attitude throughout, mediating between the two groups.

At this juncture a great fire broke out in Edo, destroying the Uesugi mansions in Sakurada and Azabu, and the idea that Yōzan had been trying to convey finally began to spread among his retainers. He maintained a modest posture, for he knew an overbearing, authoritarian attitude was not necessary to make people see reality. Yōzan did not lack courage, as he later proved when confronted with the determined opposition of seven senior retainers. His basic conviction remained: Nothing could be done unless everyone honestly acknowledged the difficult situation they were in and made a mental resolution to act in concert in grappling with the clan's financial woes.

Yōzan's efforts began to bear fruit after the fire. On their own initiative the Fifty-Horsemen Corps proposed to go into the forests themselves to cut trees and bring out the timber needed for reconstructing the mansions. Thus they became a productive labor force. Certainly the fire, an emergency for their clan, presented them with a good reason to do such work, but they would never have been so ready to plunge in without Yōzan's steadfast efforts. The timber project was a great success. Within little more than twenty days, under the direction of Takemata, more than ten thousand trees were felled and brought out of the forests. Had the clan hired inefficient day laborers instead and left its paid retainers doing nothing productive, the expenses would have been tremendous.

Yōzan took four major steps to overcome the immediate crisis: (1) through sheer frugality, he cut expenses by a large margin; (2) he cut back on wages, including his own, and excessive personnel; (3) he collected an additional tax; and (4) he made nonproductive samurai into a productive labor force. Such measures, strictly followed, would enable any nation or company about to go bankrupt to recover. One must follow the logic of capital, a principle that can apply to any society, be it capitalist, feudal capitalist, or communist—which is no more than state capitalism. Yet for most people or organizations, to see realities properly and to act on the obviously wisest course to deal with these realities, remains a difficult challenge.

A Successful Coup d'État

Yōzan's first objective was to bring the clan's finances into the black; second, to invoke the power of a law similar to the present-day Stock Company Reorganization and Rehabilitation Act to extend the term of payment of old debts; and third, to obtain fresh capital and turn the samurai into a productive labor force, in order to achieve reproduction on a progressive scale. Yōzan had never ceased his campaign to convince others of the strength of his ideas, and his thinking had begun to penetrate among his clansmen. A consensus was forming in support of it, when adamant opposition from seven senior retainers arose to put the clan on the brink of fatal internal conflict. In the seventh year after Yōzan became head of the Uesugi family, seven senior retainers, led by Suda Mitsunushi, chief retainer on duty in Edo, and Imokawa Nobuchika, went to Yonezawa castle and handed Yōzan a jointly signed document. It contained a demand that Yōzan decide on the spot whether to dismiss the Takemata Masatsuna group or the seven senior retainers, in effect, a letter of impeachment. Negotiations continued until noon the following day—literally an all-night collective bargaining session. Today doctors would stop them, but in this case Yōzan's adoptive father intervened to end the meeting by making the seven retainers withdraw.

The argument to displace Yōzan lacked a logical basis. It began with the complaint that since he assumed leadership of the domain, nothing had gone well; "poor harvests have continued year after year," undoubtedly in divine punishment for the reckless way Yōzan had plunged into new ventures, declared the letter. Calling him a "lord of the darkness," the lugubrious letter maintained that even his best efforts were useless, for "his actions being basically wrong, he is like the merchant who cares deeply about his business, but leaves the running of it to evil clerks who ruin him." (It is interesting that Yōzan's opponents also fell back on the logic of capital, comparing clan bankruptcy to that of a merchant.) The document went on to list seven points of impeachment, which can be summarized as: (1) the lord is "too concerned with trivial matters," failing to see the whole situation in a broad perspective; (2) he is served by people no better than evil clerks who should be immediately removed from their posts; (3) he should be "unobtrusive and strictly attentive to his duties" in the established tradition of the house; (4) to maintain such a low profile, he should be attended by men of honesty and impartiality; (5) he should abandon all his new policies and devote himself to sincere pursuit of the tried and true; (6) he should renounce his specious reasoning; and (7) he should rectify his erroneous practices regarding rewards and punishments, for his aides were not faithful retainers but mere flatterers.

After noting their demands, the letter—ultimatum, really—informed Yōzan that the seven retainers required an immediate answer. They declared that they would not leave the castle until he made a definite choice between themselves and his "aides." This was a threat, for they alone were present, their opponents were not. After reading the demands, Yōzan must have realized that there were only two alternatives: They would have to fall or he would.

He told them he wished to consult Shigesada, his adoptive father, but, refusing to allow even that, the seven insisted that he make his reponse then and there. When Yōzan began to question them on specific points in their case for impeachment, their answers were not clear. Debate was impossible, for their statement lacked logical substance. As the night wore on, they grew more and more overbearing, their demeanor becoming arrogant. Again they returned to their claim that because Yōzan had been adopted from the Akizuki family whose domain was worth only 30,000 *koku,* he could not possibly understand the ways of the prestigious Uesugi family and its domain of 150,000 *koku*. Throughout the night and until ten the next morning they pressed him for a decision for or against the dismissal of his assistants. Obviously a resolution of the confrontation was not in sight. Yōzan stood up; Imokawa Nobuchika, one of the seven rebellious retainers, grabbed the hem of his *hakama,* demanding the young daimyo for an answer. At that moment, Satō Hidechika, an attendant of Yōzan who had been waiting outside, rushed into the room and knocked Imokawa's hand away. Yōzan left the room to consult Shigesada. Satō alone accompanied him.

Shigesada was surprised and extremely angry to hear what had been going on. Saying that he would handle the situation, he told Yōzan to resume his place at the meeting, and then he summoned his own attendants. When Yōzan returned, the senior retainers renewed their attack with threats, warning him that if he did not decide immediately, they would file a complaint with the bakufu. Shigesada then swept into the room with his attendants. In a thunderous voice he told the seven protagonists that they should be deeply ashamed to have threatened their lord, and that he could have them executed if necessary. They finally withdrew. It was noon.

It had been a rough meeting. From then on, the seven senior retainers refused to attend their offices, claiming illness. Worse, they made it impossible for Takemata Masatsuna and other supporters of Yōzan to carry out their work. The domain government seemed to have dried up. In an attempt to compromise, Yōzan asked Shigesada's chief attendant to approach them all personally and persuade them to resume their functions, but they all refused. The seven were all of distinguished lineage in the clan, which gave them considerable influence in the domain. They also had power deriving from their official positions.

If they were to make the confrontation into a serious contest against the daimyo and his supporters, the domain would be engulfed by civil war. This is exactly what the seven were counting on, for even if head-on conflict did not develop, should the bakufu learn what was going on, it would lay the blame on Yōzan without examining the reason the trouble started.

This is why Yōzan had to act quickly. He summoned all those who had not taken sides, and learned that all of them believed that the impeachment attempt was based on unfounded accusations. With the help of this new support group, Yōzan worked out a careful plan, according to which the seven senior retainers were arrested before the bakufu could intervene. Of the seven, Suda Mitsunushi and Imokawa Nobuchika were ordered to commit ritual suicide; the others were placed in domiciliary confinement and part of their own holdings were confiscated. Warashina Rittaku, physician and Confucianist, the man who acted as advisor to the seven retainers, was executed. At last Yōzan held full power to run the domain.

Mobilizing the Jobless

Now that Yōzan held uncontested authority, he made the best use of Takemata Masatsuna's talent for management. Takemata devised a plan to raise the domain's income from 150,000 to 300,000 *koku,* virtually an income-doubling plan. But to do that, the samurai, who were "unemployed employees," had to be turned into a productive labor force. These superfluous employees, who had been mere consumers, had to be used to cultivate the land and double production.

The domain's samurai population had remained almost

the same size as in the days when the Uesugi family ran a 1,200,000 *koku* enterprise. Thus it was important above all to find ways to involve these people in productive activities. Yōzan had to overcome their psychological resistance to manual labor, which he tackled by going himself into muddy fields to plough, along with his senior retainers. He commissioned one of his attendants, Satō Bunshirō, to take charge of agricultural affairs. Satō was told even to mobilize Yōzan's favorite horse in carrying human waste for fertilizer. Takemata, too, donned a straw raincoat and ploughed the fields. His family, outraged, declared that it was a disgrace "for a domain leader to engage in such indecent work," but Takemata replied angrily that he had not a qualm about "taking up a sickle in the hand meant to bear a sword, and muddying my feet" as long as such work would help the domain in an emergency. Glowing with the spirit that was beginning to grip everyone, Takemata reveled in the drudgery, declaring that nothing could express more eloquently a samurai's determination to overcome the crisis.

Suzuki Shōsan said many times, "Agricultural labor is Buddhist practice." In the case of the Yonezawa clan, agricultural labor had become the expression of loyalty to the lord. The *Buke shichitoku,* a treatise on the seven virtues of the samurai written in 1845, describes the revolution. "All the retainers in the clan, high-ranking or low-ranking, offered to work, and putting on straw raincoats and bamboo hats, and taking sickles and hoes in hand, they cultivated fields that had lain fallow for several years. A year later these had become productive fields." Takemata also organized a tree nursery. It had three parts, one for lacquer trees, another for mulberry, and the third for *kōzo* (paper mulberry) trees. His plan included planting a million trees in each part.

Once Yōzan and his supporters had a general idea of how income and expenditures could be balanced through hard work and frugality, their next move was to approach the "money parents." Takemata asked Mitani Sankurō, one of the Yonezawa clan's money parents in Edo, to send his assistant to Yonezawa. He showed him around, so that the assistant might see what was going on. After telling him all about the domain, Takemata described their plans for the future and asked for financial assistance. Takemata then went to Kansai to meet the clan's money parents there, with whom he set about negotiating a temporary suspension of old debts and repayment in yearly installments, and he tried to gain exemption from interest. In place of interest, Takemata offered the money parents a stipend in rice. Such arrangements were often made between feudal lords and merchants, for the merchants judged it highly advantageous to receive a semipermanent rice stipend. Mitsui Takafusa warned that such promises made by samurai or daimyo were not reliable and the money lent would most likely be irrecoverable, but he added that if the promise were kept, both merchant and borrower would benefit. Takemata finally succeeded in having the old debts amortized and getting new, low-interest loans from Mitani Sankurō.

Takemata knew that exporting manufactured goods, which have a high value added, would be much more profitable than selling raw materials to other provinces, but the production and sale of such goods also require considerable investment. He used every possible means to obtain financing, and then concentrated his efforts on turning raw materials into finished products. At the time, Nara was well known for its bleached cotton cloth, and Ojiya (Niigata) for its crepe. Both were made from ramie produced in Yonezawa. Capitalizing on the opportunity,

Takemata invited some of the Ojiya craftsmen to Yone-zawa and built a crepe factory. He also set up an office to oversee the development of an indigo-dyeing industry and invited experts from Sendai to make tests on cultivating the indigo plant. The results were so good that he ordered the plant to be cultivated widely throughout the domain, and he prohibited the import of any indigo from outside. All indigo produced within the domain was bought up by the clan, which then sold it to dyers. The list of similar achievements would fill an entire volume.

But not everything went smoothly. In any society, in any period, someone in power for a long time will inevitbly gather all sorts of people around him. Not all of them are good and wise, as Takemata was to discover. The economy of a given community is no more than a means to other ends, and as soon as economic measures bring some results, people think of those achievements as the natural consequences of their own work. They do not appreciate those who made and carried out the measures. The Japanese economy grew rapidly under Ikeda Hayato (prime minister from 1960 to 1964), whose successful income-doubling plan and rapid growth policies were the hallmark of his administration. But he is almost forgotten today. At one point, he was hit by a harsh backlash when critics attacked his policies as the source of all Japan's evils. "Down with the GNP!" was the popular call for a time.

It was no different two hundred years ago in the Yone-zawa domain. The more successful Takemata's "double income" program proved to be, the more difficult his position became. In 1777 he offered to resign, but was not permitted to do so. Three years later he once again volunteered to resign, but again without success. The people working under him had formed a powerful faction, making Takemata their boss; and these people could not allow their boss to resign lest it weaken their own faction. Thus they pressed Yōzan not to accept Takemata's resignation. Then, quite suddenly, in 1782 he was ordered to resign and was confined to a house that once belonged to the Imokawa family. He seemed to have been expecting this, and followed the order calmly. Yōzan did not confiscate his land but let Takemata's son inherit it. Why this happened is not clear, but Yōzan may have decided that the only way to release Takemata from his position was to order him out of office.

The Great Legacy

Yōzan's activities ranged far beyond just economic policies. He expanded social welfare and educational facilities, just as today's large corporations are doing for their employees. This was only natural, for the feudal domain was a social and human community as well as a functional group or economic organization. A severe famine that hit Japan the year after Takemata's resignation proved how foresighted Yōzan's reforms had been. In those days, the *han* was an independent economic entity, and it was none of its business whether other domains went bankrupt or were ruined. Today, an employee uses such terms as "our company," "our humble company," or "our inconsequential company" in reference to his own firm, while he says "your honorable company" or "your noble firm" when speaking of others. In the Tokugawa period, too, people spoke of "our humble *han*" and "your worthy *han*," which simply demonstrates the distant, formal relations that existed among them.

If one domain was suffering from famine and another had surplus grain, the one with the surplus rarely helped the starving domain. The great famine of 1783 was most severe in the northeast. People were forced to eat straw and pine bark, dog and cat meat. In the Nanbu domain some ate human corpses. But Yonezawa *han* had ample grain in stock, and it could even afford to obtain more from Sakata and the vicinity of Echigo. Moreover, the unusual weather that had prevailed since the beginning of the year told them that the crop would be poor, and so the *han* had been as frugal as possible. No one starved to death and no families were broken up in Yonezawa. The weather was bad the following year as well, and by the end of the year, the entire stock of grain, carefully collected and stored by all available means since 1774 when Yōzan finally acquired full power, had been exhausted. Thereupon Yōzan began a long-term plan to create a stock inventory of 150,000 *hyō* of grain within the next twenty years.

This brief examination of the economic policies of a typical enlightened daimyo, who was a skillful economic manager in the Tokugawa period, provides a good case study, for such diamyo were numerous at the time. There were some daimyo who gave up trying to run their domains and abandoned the effort entirely. *Edo kenbun niroku* (Two cases inspected in Edo) contains the following passage:

> The act of selling and leaving one's house and land due to extreme poverty is called *urisue*. Recently it is reported, a lord resorted to *urisue*. He was the lord of a small fief of 70,000 *koku*. Officially he claims to have adopted an heir and retired, but he sold to the heir all the family belongings, stipend, and even retainers, for 3,000 *kin*. He himself is living secretly in a mansion outside the domain. There could be none of the usual father-child relations between him and his adopted son. Even if a lord tried to sell his fief, the retainers would not let him do so. But it seems that in this case, both the lord and his retainers are satisfied—one wonders why. Such retainers are not loyal. . . .

A fief of 70,000 *koku* was certainly small, but Yonezawa *han,* having only double that amount, was by no means big. Without the bold but prudent management of Yōzan, the domain would probably have been brought to the same ignominy. In *Keizairoku shūi* (Gleanings from economic records), Dazai Shundai describes the other daimyo who were very good managers:

> Today there are still *han* that continue to augment their income by carrying on trade begun a long time ago. The lord of Tsushima has a small domain with a yield of only slightly more than 20,000 *koku*. But he buys ginseng root and many other items from Korea, and has kept a monopoly on those Korean goods, which he sells to other domains at very high prices. He is now wealthier than a lord whose fief brings 200,000 *koku*. The Matsumae domain is a small fief of 7,000 *koku* in Hokkaido, but the clan is richer than the lord of a 50,000 *koku* domain. Lord Tsuwano in the province of Iwami had a domain worth 40,000 *koku,* but sales of cardboard manufactured by the clan bring the total income to a level comparable to a domain with a fief of 150,000 *koku*. Lord Hamaguchi in the same province followed Lord Tsuwano's example and began producing cardboard; his domain's income has doubled. . . . Study their economy and carry out carefully made plans. All domains, large and small, have their own special products. . . . Those with few special products should train their people in other industries and continually urge them to work. Besides the various grains, they should plant whatever useful trees and grasses will grow on their land, in order to create more special products.

What Dazai is saying is that the managerial ability to raise productivity is of utmost importance.

The Tokugawa period was a time when everyone, from lord to commoner, was made to learn economy and to understand that those who did not follow the logic of capital would be ruined. The conditions of the period also taught them that unless the ethics of capitalism were practiced as well, the logic of capital itself would collapse. While Baigan taught a practical workers' ethic, Yōzan and other enlightened lords taught the ethics of management. These traditions remain today. To learn that the president of Keidanren lives modestly, and that the chairman of All Nippon Airways lives in the same kind of house as an ordinary middle-class family is deeply impressive to Japanese, and they put their trust in such people. If they wish for long-term success, those who have charge of corporations that are closely bound to the political and economic life of the Japanese nation—corporations that remind us of the old *han*-run enterprises, they must abide by the same strict, self-denying ethics of capital practiced by the "wise" lords of the Tokugawa period. In short, those in management must be unselfish and unavaricious as they pursue the logic of capital. It is an ethic unique in the human history, comparable to the Puritan ethic of Western civilization.

Yamato Yūzō once wrote of an interesting episode. When asked by Japanese reporters "Who is your favorite Japanese," the late U.S. president John F. Kennedy answered, "Yōzan." Few of the reporters had ever heard of Yōzan. Apparently, Americans too are attracted to this kind of person. How can we sum up Yōzan's attitude? More than anything, he makes a sharp distinction between public and private. Throughout his career, he showed a grasp of the logic of capital on the public level. Consider the following three precautions he passed on to his successor:

1. Do not make the state (domain) your property, for it is something that is transmitted from ancestors to descendants.

2. Do not make the people your property, for they belong to the state.

3. You exist for the state and the people, not vice versa.

Where such thinking is lacking, there can be no modern state. This concept, articulated by Yōzan, is still alive in Japanese corporations. It is the legacy of what should be called "Han, Inc.," a proud tradition that has made Japan what it is today.

8

ECONOMIC EFFICIENCY AND
THE CAPITALIST ETHIC

For the townsmen of the Tokugawa period, the logic of capital, described in the previous chapter, was nothing new. What they needed was a capitalist ethic, and this was articulated by Ishida Baigan. For the warrior class, the ethic of the samurai was transformed into the capitalist ethic; it was the *logic* of capital that they lacked. Uesugi Yōzan and other enlightened daimyo of the Tokugawa period supplied this need, through their example as outstanding managers.

The ideas taught by Baigan and practiced by the wise lords have a common source in the concept of "labor as religious practice," as defined by the samurai-turned-priest Suzuki Shōsan. Baigan was thus justified in arguing that the same principles applied to all of the four classes of feudal society: samurai, peasants, artisans, and merchants. Shōsan wrote in *Shimin nichiyō* (Daily life of the four classes) that the difference between the four classes was mainly a functional one, and this ultimately became the basis of the movement of "equality of the four classes" (*shimin byōdō*) that emerged in the Meiji period. Shōsan believed that labor based on the pursuit of economic rationality without thought of personal gain was good, and that labor had intrinsic value, be it for the lord of a domain or a merchant. Baigan and Yōzan shared this idea, and it typified the mentality with which Japan entered the Meiji period and that enabled the nation to overcome successfully the utter destruction it suffered in World War II.

Shōsan, Baigan, and Yōzan considered labor noble and productive activity sacred. This attitude toward work characterizes many of the owners of small and medium-sized enterprises in the postwar period described in earlier chapters. In the Edo period, the main form of productive activity was farming, and thus agriculture tended to be considered especially noble. Shōsan himself considered both manufacturing and trade vocations as honorable as farming; he was not an advocate of narrow, agrarian fundamentalist thinking.

Yōzan recognized the merit of high value-added commodities, and took capital financing and interest on investments for granted. He could hardly be called an agrarian fundamentalist either. In his day, however, buying and selling as an occupation was widely despised, and it was especially looked down on by the proponents of the ideology of samurai superiority, even though as a class their fundamental raison d'être had been virtually eliminated by the continuing peace. As mentioned earlier, followers of the orthodox Confucianism of the day also looked askance at commercial activity. This mentality was a product of the insularity and absence of strife of the Tokugawa period.

Aida Yūji, historian, calls such people "true believers" of the worst kind. Their arguments were unrealistic, for their own profession had been rendered meaningless; yet they strove valiantly to maintain their social status on the strength of a moral principle. Their pronouncements were invariably radical, although in fact they feared nothing more than reform and clung desperately to outmoded principles to validate their existence. Aida believes they resembled the radicals in the Chinese Cultural Revolution who accepted without question the teachings of Mao Zedong. The intraclan strife of the Edo period between the advocates of the orthodox line, or "principle," and the capitalist-line samurai who supported and strove for economic rationalism reminds us of the struggle in China between the "red" and the "expert." In Japan the ultimate outcome of this struggle was the Meiji Restoration.

Whichever position they held, neither side in the Tokugawa period regarded agricultural labor as contemptible. Yōzan treated it as a matter of course that his favorite horse be used to help carry human waste for fertilizer. Takemata Masatsuna, one of his senior retainers, put aside his sword, took up a plow, and waded into the mud to cultivate the fields, declaring that such toil for the sake of the domain was something a samurai should be proud of.

This tradition is still alive. A serial television drama broadcast by Japan Broadcasting Corporation in 1979 entitled *Mā nēchan* (Big sister Mā) (original story by Hasegawa Machiko, writer of popular comics such as the *Sazaesan* series and the *Ijiwaru bāsan* series) is a good illustration. The drama, based on the experiences of Hasegawa and her family, centers around the elder sister, to whom she was especially attached. One program in the series showed how family members would go out to gather horse dung in the streets to use as fertilizer for their vegetable garden. It was wartime and everyone cultivated vegetable gardens to help make up for the shortage of food. But one day when they went out to gather manure, they found that someone had come and beat them to the valuable quarry. Thus began a race to be the "early bird," reducing them all to nervous wrecks before the affair was over.

I was fascinated by this television program because of its similarity to a story I once read in the *Yomiuri shimbun* published on January 1, 1876 (Meiji 9). This account, entitled "Night Soil Thief," went as follows:

> It was a veritable tempest in a teapot. On the fourth day of the month, all the households of the number 24 block of 4-chome Bakurochō, formerly the location of an Edo officer's mansion, discovered that the night soil had been removed—stolen—from the sewers of every single residence in the neighborhood. "It's all very well to clean the sewers for us," the local headman fumed, "but what an execrable thief!"

Although the incident involved a crime of theft, the newspaper was clearly in sympathy with the thief, and reported it humorously.

The story of Hasegawa Machiko was set at a time more than thirty years ago, and that of the night soil thief a century ago. It matters little that in one case the coveted item was "collected," and in the other "stolen." The point is that they were both cases of "refuse collection without permission" in which the substance in question was valuable enough to warrant certain extraordinary efforts in obtaining it; and both happened during periods of great hardship. If he had been caught, the night soil thief might have been ashamed to have been stealing, but certainly not because of the prize he was after.

Many Japanese had experiences during World War II similar to that of Hasegawa Machiko, but they are not the least bit embarrassed by them. On the contrary, they are proud of the ingenuity and tenacity they had in coping with difficult times. Gathering human or animal waste for fertilizer is nothing unusual in Japan, but what would happen, for example, if a report of such an incident were to be broadcast on television in India? The response would be entirely different. No doubt the person involved, whether he had been collecting or stealing, would have been shunned as an untouchable. There is a story of the wife of a Japanese executive living in India who, unsatisfied with the way a maid was dusting her house, took up the duster and showed the maid how she wanted it done. From that moment on, however, all the servants ceased obeying their mistress's orders, concluding that she must come from the lowest caste in Japanese society.

In India, a person like Yōzan, who ordered his own horse to be put to work carrying human waste for fertilizer in order to encourage his people to work hard, would have been despised and ridiculed by all. It is not surprising that a capitalist society like that of Japan should not emerge there.

The Challenge of Crisis

In both the early years of the Meiji period and those immediately after World War II the country was so poor that even night soil became something worth stealing. Overall, living standards in Japan have been relatively high, but in these two periods, they were no higher than that of any other country in Asia today. It was not only the populace who had to struggle for their very survival; the government, too, was on the verge of bankruptcy, and the situation was worse than in Yonezawa when Yōzan became head of the Uesugi clan. To judge from the fiscal condition of the newly established Meiji government, one might even have questioned whether it deserved the name. Indeed, it appeared more like a parasite of the wealthy merchant houses like the Mitsui. Immediately after the end of World War II, both the government and the people were in equally strapped circumstances. Production in the mining and manufacturing industries for August 1945 was a tenth of what it had been per month between 1934 and 1936, a year before the outbreak of the second Sino-Japanese war that eventually led Japan into the Pacific War. Agricultural production in 1945 had decreased to 60 percent of the prewar figure. The bombings had burned to ashes 119 cities, almost every metropolis in the country, excluding Kyoto, Nara, Hirosaki, and a few others. The people had virtually no stores of daily necessities. In addition, seven million Japanese repatriots returned from overseas with few possessions save what they carried with them. Not surprisingly, many predicted that ten million people would starve to death.

In Korea, I once met a Korean soldier who had been trained in the Imperial army. He said that the period after the Korean War had been terrible in Korea, but no more terrible than the post-Pacific War period in Japan. What made it possible for Japanese to rebuild their nation from such utter chaos, he declared, was something the most sophisticated computer would never be able to figure out.

The situation at the beginning of the Meiji era, as Japan emerged from its long isolation from the rest of the world, was, in some ways, different from that after World War II. At the close of the Tokugawa period Japan had management know-how but lacked new technology, while with defeat in the Pacific War, it had considerable technology accumulated since the Meiji Restoration, but had lost all its capital and equipment in the war. Yet in both periods, Japanese were keenly aware that they lagged behind other nations of the world, and they plunged with equal determination and energy into the task of acquiring new technology, new scientific knowledge, and new institutions and methods from Europe and the United States. Both in early Meiji and in the early postwar period, Japanese intuitively recognized that all they needed to build on the know-how and experience they already had was the modern, advanced technology of the West. They knew they had to get it even if it meant a certain period of deprivation and difficulty. The situation they faced called for extraordinary effort, the kind that people can only achieve when they confront a crisis at its worst extremity.

The intensity of the effort is eloquently expressed in the statement presented by Inoue Kaoru and Shibusawa Eiichi in 1873 as they resigned from the Ministry of Finance in opposition to the conservatives in control of the government, excerpted as follows:

> Who that loves his country does not want to make its government as civilized as that of the countries of the West? Today no government official who has ever glimpsed the West through translated books or pictures, though he may never have seen conditions in foreign countries at first hand, can fail to take up the challenge of building his nation to a standard equal to that of Western countries. How much more intensely do those who have actually traveled overseas feel the desire to reach this goal.
>
> Among those who return from abroad, some say England is the most superior nation; others say it is France, still others the Netherlands, the United States, Prussia, or Austria. They cite how much better than in Japan is everything in those countries, not only their cities, their currencies, land reclamation methods, and commerce, but their armies, scholarship, parliamentary processes, laws, steam and electrical power, clothing, and machines. For the advancement of our civilization, they declare that Japan must emulate the West in all these things. Their sentiments are perfectly natural, and because they believe this out of love for their nation, they cannot be denied.
>
> Yet if the form of things is given too great an emphasis and the substance is neglected, government will go against its people; institutions will thrive while the people are impoverished; and living standards may rise while the strength of the nation withers.

For all the merits of foreign things, the nation itself would risk
bankruptcy before it has even seen success. . . .

This passage vividly reveals the combination of desperate haste and anxiety felt by Japanese in the early years of
the Meiji era. They lagged behind the West as a result of
the three hundred years of "stagnation" during Tokugawa
rule; they had to make up for lost time immediately, and
Western culture, institutions, and technology had to be
adopted no matter what the sacrifice. As mentioned above,
the country was so poor as to make even night soil an
object worth stealing, but the desire to catch up with the
West was intense, even though the reality was that fulfillment of this desire might completely exhaust the overbur-
dened populace. They faced the very real possibility that
the nation itself might collapse before their goal could be
achieved. The situation in the 1870s and 1880s was almost
exactly like that right after the end of World War II, when
priority production was instituted to rehabilitate the country.

Facing Reality Comes First

Conditions must have seemed very difficult at that time.
But we must question whether the comparison the Meiji
people made between the West they glimpsed in transla-
tions and pictures and the Japan that they knew was an
accurate one. Was the three hundred years of the Tokugawa
period really a period of stagnation? Was Japan really
"backward" compared with the West? If we take an objective look at the Tokugawa period, we find that it was by
no means a period of stagnation. On the contrary, Japan
made a great deal of progress during that time. The

direction of that progress was naturally different from that in the West, but in the field of education, for example, it was in no way inferior to the West. The period was not intellectually quiescent either, as illustrated by the development of thought from Suzuki Shōsan and Ishida Baigan to Fuse Shōō, who developed Baigan's philosophy into a sort of theory of evolution, and Kamata Ryūō, who built a mechanistic view of the cosmos on the basis of Baigan's thought. Baigan's lectures were open to everyone regardless of social status or sex, and although men and women were seated separately, his academy was essentially coeducational. Economic rationality was something understood at the time, and the ethic that validated the pursuit of economic rationality had also become established, gradually permeating throughout society from the well-educated ruling class to the lower ranks of samurai and among the townspeople as well.

True, a technological gap existed between Japan and the West, but Japan had a versatile and diligent work force that was fully capable of adopting mechanical methods of production whenever they might be introduced. The people regarded labor, if anything, as a kind of religious practice, not as something degrading or dishonorable as thought by the upper strata of society in earlier times. Townspeople managed their businesses according to rational principles, and "wise" daimyo, setting the example themselves, demonstrated that even the governing of a domain was impossible without observing the principles of economic rationality.

A revolution generally leads to the rejection of everything that went before it. The Meiji government, naturally, took this stance: The Tokugawa period was the "dark ages" and the Meiji Restoration was the "dawn of a new civilization." Whenever things went wrong, it justified itself by casting the blame on the former bakufu government. This attitude has led Japanese to many mistaken judgments about their own nation, some of which have not been corrected even today. It is also the source of the notion that Japanese are nothing but imitators and incapable of creating anything original through the process of trial and error.

But far from being a period of inertia and stagnation, the Tokugawa period witnessed an immense amount of painstaking trial and error. The leaders of domains that had most skillfully managed their affairs, "enriching their lands and strengthening their arms," were the ones who held the reins of the new Meiji government. Having already tried and tested policies within their own domains, they needed only to apply the lessons they had learned on these "pilot projects" on the national scale in "enriching the nation and strengthening its arms."

Among the domains that took the lead in creating the Meiji government were Satsuma and Chōshū, both of which had experienced recent defeat in war. Satsuma had waged a brief war against England in 1863, and the Chōshū clan the following year had fought the combined fleet of England, France, the United States, and the Netherlands. In the former war, British bombardments had reduced the port city of Kagoshima to ashes much as the B-29s were to level Tokyo less than a century later; in the latter struggle, enemy troops had landed on Chōshū, occupying part of the domain for a time. It was men from these two clans, which had felt the might of the Western powers close at hand, who led the Meiji government. In this sense, the Meiji government might be likened to the post-World War II Japanese government. Japan in both periods was like a corporation facing a crisis for lack of up-to-date technology that has also been burned out because of war. The Japanese enterprise was such that it needed only to install new, efficient equipment and institute the necessary organizational reforms in order to restore immediately its business performance.

Viewed this way, the success of the Meiji reforms was no miracle, nor was the reconstruction of the country after World War II. Just as the people of Meiji had gritted their teeth for a "last-ditch effort" to achieve modernization and maintain national autonomy, postwar Japanese coped with the difficulties and deprivation of their defeated nation with methods such as priority production. To pull itself out of the ruins of war, Japan had to start producing raw materials. To accomplish this it had to increase production of its sole source of energy at the time—coal. This was self-evident, but at the time production had fallen to 23 million tons. Before the war, 60 percent of coal production had gone into industry, while 40 percent had been consumed by railways, ships, and households. Demand in the latter categories was relatively inflexible, and so, when coal production dropped, it was the demand in industry that invariably had to give way. With only 23 million tons of coal being produced, only 9.4 million tons could go for industrial use, far too little to raise raw material production and thus facilitate rehabilitation.

Coal production had to be raised to 30 million tons, and to make this possible, steel materials were a prerequisite. Production of steel in 1945 was practically nil—only 550,000 tons and less than a tenth of what it had been in 1934 and 1935. The drastic drop in steel production was caused by the shortage of coal. This vicious circle could not be destroyed without cutting down on nonindustrial use of coal as much as possible and channeling more coal into production of steel, which could then be used to raise coal output. It required the people to manage with only the scantiest supplies of coal and other sources of energy. It was a time, like the early Meiji period, that called for extraordinary effort to get through the crisis—to "endure the unendurable" even if it meant starvation. Japanese faced the stern fact that they could not do otherwise and hope their situation would improve. As we observed in the story of Uesugi Yōzan's struggle to save his domain, the most difficult part is to see things objectively—to face reality. Yet once reality is grasped for what it is, the problem is practically solved. In both the early Meiji and immediate postwar periods, there were those who could not accept the hardships and were strongly opposed to making such great sacrifices. But despite the inevitable turmoil, the majority of Japanese were capable of seeing things objectively. In every age there are propagandists who may succeed in temporarily persuading people to follow them, but once they ignore economic rationality, their following falls away, a lesson the whole Japanese nation learned, in a sense, from the Pacific War. The Tokugawa period had taught a similar lesson.

Bad Management Brings Its Own Downfall

In both these times of trial, those who ignored the principles of economic rationality and went bankrupt were not looked on as victims of circumstances beyond their control, but as victims of their own folly. Those who managed to survive difficult times by observing the rules of economic rationality were admired. After World War II, as in the early days of Meiji, there were many bankruptcies, but what is notable is people's attitudes toward those whose businesses failed. Let us compare two accounts published in 1874, one concerning the House of Ono and the other the House of Mitsui, both of which were then among the largest merchant-banking firms in Japan. The article on the Ono appeared in the *Tokyo Nichinichi shimbun* on November 23, and gives us a good idea of the response of the press to conditions at the time.

> The well-known House of Ono closed its doors on November 20. Founded by the Ono family under the leadership of Ono Zensuke, it has been responsible since the time of the Meiji Restoration for handling the financial affairs of the Imperial court together with the House of Mitsui. The Ono ranked shoulder-to-shoulder with Mitsui in the Japanese business world, and was such a solid concern that everyone believed it would eternally prosper. To hear so suddenly that it has ceased business comes as a shock almost beyond belief.

The article begins in this sympathetic tone, but it soon becomes apparent that the writer considers it inevitable that a company that has not obeyed the rules of economic rationality will fail.

> The unexpected closing of the House of Ono may come as a surprise, but on careful thought, it was probably only the natural course of events. One even begins to wonder that it did not happen long ago.
>
> Most of the wealthy families in Japan are headed by people with little talent. They are merely the inheritors of estates accumulated by their forebears, and most leave the management of family affairs entirely up to their senior clerks. Although mere townsmen, they put on airs like daimyo, and even the real daimyo lost their status in 1871 with the abolition of the domains and the establishment of the prefectural system. It goes against all common sense that a merchant family could maintain wealth and a good name for centuries without competent leadership. Indeed, many thousands of old and wealthy families in Tokyo, Osaka, and other parts of Japan have gone bankrupt or broken up within the past four or five years, and without exception, these are families whose heads lack the aptitude for business and whose

senior clerks, although given total authority for family affairs, are oblivious to the economic realities of the times. Out of sympathy we must feel sorry for them, but reason tells us that their bankruptcies were inevitable.

Some may argue that the businesses that went bankrupt in early Meiji were unfortunate victims unable to cope with the tremendous changes brought about by the Restoration. But if a company goes bankrupt, it is its managers, not the government, who must take the blame. This is not merely my own opinion; it has been a fundamental part of Japanese thinking since the Tokugawa period that a business that ignores the rules of economic rationality will fail. Even the Japanese newspapers, who are in the habit of blaming the government for almost anything, do not attribute corporate bankruptcies to the government. On this point the Japanese press has been consistent ever since the start of the Meiji era, and it is a sound attitude shared by all Japanese even today.

On the other hand, a company that is managed efficiently as a functional group and which, as a kind of cooperative group, divides its profits among its members, was highly praised. On May 15, 1874, the *Yūbin hōchi* newspaper carried the article, "Wealthy House of Mitsui Apportions Profits Among Employees: Highest Bonus ¥15,000 [at contemporary value of yen]," which read in part as follows:

The House of Mitsui has rendered distinguished service to the Emperor since the time of the Restoration, as is well known among the Japanese people. From the first year of Meiji (1868) until the present, it has made financial assistance available to government ministries and prefectural governments, and has recently accrued profit on its investments. Today it shared these profits among its employees from the first to thirteeth ranks,

including the well-known Mr. Minomura. Personnel of the first
rank received ¥15,000 or more, and those in the twelfth rank
received no less than ¥500. Reports are that the Mitsui profits are
the result of its great efforts in works in the public interest with
little concern for private gain, and the family is managed so well
that people are quick to cooperate with it.

Quite apart from the accuracy of the facts reported, it is
clear from the context of the article that the newspaper is
applauding the Mitsui for the profits it has gained through
efficient management of its affairs and for dividing the
profits among the members of the Mitsui group. Considered along with the article on the House of Ono, we can
see that the evaluations of both firms reflect quite faithfully
the principles taught by Suzuki Shōsan and Ishida Baigan
in the Tokugawa period. They are evidence that the ideas
of these thinkers were alive and well in the thinking of
Meiji Japanese.

Japanese believe in the logic of capital, and have little
patience with those who ignore economic rationality.
Once they see that a course of action promises future
development in accordance with the principles of economic rationalism, they will willingly follow it even if it
requires great sacrifice. This is why, I believe, the oil
shocks and energy shortages were not really serious problems for Japan. We have survived much greater crises. If
there is any truly fearsome trouble for Japan, it would be
the loss of this very tradition.

There will always be people of the kind that Aida Yūji
called "true believers," who cling to established ethical
values. They, too, represent a certain tradition, which has
arisen with indignation to defend the capitalist ethic every
time it has been violated since the Tokugawa period. Both
in the early period of Japan's modernization in the nineteenth century and in the postwar era, there were cases in

which the logic of capitalism was allowed to overwhelm the capitalist ethic, as symbolized by the all too frequent political scandals. As the newspaper articles quoted above show, Japanese are discerning judges of economic efficiency and managerial competence, and they have little sympathy for those who violate the ethical rules of society. This is something that both political leaders and corporate management must keep in mind, for public feeling against unethical conduct can be so strong in Japan as to divert the fundamental direction of national policy, the consequences for which they have only themselves to blame.

Haste Makes Waste

Denunciation of unethical activity has become a given in Japanese society and without it Japanese capitalism would collapse. But economic rationality, pursued with such single-minded haste that it works against, not for investment in the future, is equally condemnable. A clear distinction must be made between economic efficiency and investment in the future. To criticize or ignore an investment in the future out of narrow concern with economic efficiency may later prove to be mistaken. An example of the kind of criticism that grows out of too great a concern for economic efficiency appeared in the May 12, 1874, issue of the *Nisshin shinjishi,* a newspaper run by an Englishman in Japan, in an article entitled "Attack on the Japanese Lack of Consistency":

> The *Yokohama shimbun* says that a great amount of money was wasted over four years in building a railroad line. It extends only twenty-five miles, and the construction is poor. Electric lines were raised, but affixed so ineptly that they are in need of constant

repair. Yet all of these efforts receive excessive praise, leading us to lose all faith in the Japanese government. Why is this so? . . . In China things are very different from in Japan . . . there is less blind pursuit of novelty and obsession with new things; there is less adopting of haphazard policies that leave the people confused about what is happening, and less of the proclivity to plunge into big projects without adequately gauging the real strength of the country, thus driving the populace into flood and fire. That is why business grows more and more prosperous in China and more and more sluggish in Japan. Why must Japan alone be so excessive!

This is the kind of criticism that grows out of too great a concern with economic efficiency in the immediate future. The tendency in the Japanese press to lavish praise on the Great Cultural Revolution in China and criticize the economic growth policies of the Japanese government grows out of the same argument. It is also why Japanese vehemently oppose the construction of nuclear power plants; they are so impatient that they see only the immediate effects of adopting new technology.

The pursuit of economic rationality, which has a long tradition from the Tokugawa period, thus has both advantages and disadvantages. What we must do is to reassess this tradition and take measures to make the most of its advantages for the future.

9

THE TRADITION OF JAPANESE CAPITALISM

In the previous chapters of this book I have gone into some detail in discussing the peculiar features of Japanese capitalism, but mine is not what is generally considered academic work. I am not a scholar, nor am I what Ishida Baigan would call a "learned geisha." I do not want to publish bombastic theories simply for the sake of making my ideas known. But I have ideals. Born and bred in the Japanese tradition, I believe in the unbroken order of the universe that gives us life and breath. Because this is a positive credo, I could never follow an ideology that condoned the death of millions of my fellow countrymen. It would be unbearable to me if my compatriots were forced out of their land as "boat people," to almost certain death by drowning. In short, I believe in whatever will allow the Japanese nation to exist in peace, its companies to prosper in peace, and every individual to live in peace. This book would be useless if it did not in some way support the ideals I hold.

Insofar as a social structure is a reflection of the mind-set of the people in that society, whatever is of value to the individual should also be of value to the corporate body of which he or she is part, and by extension, to the entire nation. Not everyone would agree with this view, but there are facts to back it up, as we can see in a brief review of the discussion presented in the preceding chapters.

By the early Tokugawa period, it had become axiomatic that nothing could last very long without economic rationality; no individual, no merchant, no domain could survive, much less succeed, if the "logic of capital" was ignored. No one doubted that the pursuit of rationality was good. For Ishida Baigan, thorough rationalization in the consumer's interest was the hallmark of "honest business." The lord of Yonezawa, Uesugi Yōzan, had no qualms about putting his favorite horse to work hauling human waste to the fields for fertilizer, insofar as this fertilizer helped raise the economic efficiency of the domain management. Nor did Uesugi's senior retainer, Takemata Masatsuna, disdain taking up a hoe and wading into the paddy fields. These men were not motivated by the pursuit of personal gain, but by concern for their community or their domain. Baigan remonstrated against any impulse for personal gain; for him, commerce was a vocation, intended to serve society, to support the communal entity that was the merchant house, and to guarantee the livelihood of its members.

The basic principle underlying these ideas was that the communal group—in the cases presented, the domain—must be a functional group that operates according to the logic of capital, and that the merchant house, in order to be a functional group, must also be a communal group. This principle, I believe, is what enabled Japan to achieve what has been called "miraculous" development, both in the Meiji era and after World War II. Such a measure of success, on a national scale, meant that every individual understood and had assimilated this principle, and belief in it took various forms of expression. Suzuki Shōsan said "agricultural labor is Buddhist practice," indeed, that all work is Buddhist practice. One should seek fulfillment through work itself; work provides religious and spiritual satisfaction. If one approaches work in this way, no task is too demeaning. In the Tokugawa period, hoeing the fields or gathering horse manure was not below even a samurai, if the situation was critical enough.

On the organizational level, when the individual performs a role as a member of a functional group, that individual is also serving the communal group that forms the functional group, and this is the source of spiritual fulfillment. Thus, it is natural that an enduring organization will center on an object of corporate worship, focus on a corporate objective, or be led by a charismatic personality that embodies certain objectives. And because the group is a communal one, employment is naturally for life, and a system of seniority exists in one form or another, although employment is not governed by contracts.

These assumptions gave rise to practices that undeniably have functioned very successfully in Japan. Self-control and frugality, which is a manifestation of self-control, provide the basis for social order. Frugality, considered a responsibility to society, underlies the imperative to conserve energy, and the strong consciousness of the need for energy conservation will continue to work to Japan's advantage. Economist Hasegawa Keitarō was undoubtedly right when he said that even if the price of oil rose to $40 a barrel, Japan would continue to prosper.

The people of the Tokugawa period knew very well how limited their natural resources were, a fact of life felt all the more starkly in the confined, semiclosed world of the feudal domain. They had to make do with what was at hand, and they had no choice but to be frugal. Frugality

became an established moral principle of individual conduct. Luxury was a vice; it spelled the breakdown of order.

Bankruptcy Is a Necessary Evil

That which is an advantage can quickly become a disadvantage. This is true for the state, for a corporation, and
for the individual. A functional group that is also a communal group has certain advantages, as long as it is working properly. If its direction should go astray, however, it
may end up functioning solely for the maintenance of the
communal group. The Imperial Japanese Army is an example of such a development in recent history. Today, the
so-called 3 Ks (*kome,* literally "rice," referring to the
governmental system of food controls; *kenkō hoken,* the
national health insurance program; and Kokutetsu, the
Japan National Railways (JNR), formerly a public corporation) are the three most deficit-ridden institutions in the
Japanese government. Because they are not functioning
well, they are struggling to stay afloat—just to keep the
communal group intact. An army is an organization
whose function is to protect the lives and property of a
nation's citizens, but when an army becomes a communal
group too, it may also be transformed into a system that
exploits the lives and property of citizens in order to
maintain its own existence. That is what happened to the
Imperial Japanese Army, eventually bringing Japan's
downfall in the Pacific War.

To elaborate on the current example of the Japan National Railways, this mammoth enterprise was established
as a functional group for the purpose of transportation.
Today it is functioning solely to maintain the communal
group known as the "JNR Family." The deficits that arise

from its inefficient operations are covered by taxes paid by Japanese citizens. Nōkyō (the nationwide network of agricultural cooperatives) is another institution of such a communal nature. Basically, the role of the farmer is to supply the people with agricultural products. If one follows Baigan's thinking, he is expected to be "honest" and "good" in making products available at the lowest prices possible through a thoroughly efficient system. Our agricultural cooperatives, however, sell rice to the government at prices several times higher than the international price of rice, and naturally it is the taxpayers who must absorb the difference.

Clearly, Japanese have not made the best of painful experiences. Even today, as in the cases of the JNR and Nōkyō, maintaining the communal entity too often gains highest priority, and the matter of for whom the system is functioning is reduced to secondary importance. This is the greatest dilemma of groups in Japan that are at once communal and functional.

Overcoming this dilemma demands a rigorous observance of the logic of capital and the kind of no-nonsense, even cold-blooded view of bankruptcy that we saw in the story of the House of Ono in the previous chapter. The Ono merchant establishment had indeed made an important contribution to the Meiji Restoration, but any concern that ignores the basic rules of economy faces inevitable backruptcy. Here again we see how the advantages of the functional-as-communal group can become disadvantages.

By the same logic, overprotection of certain taxpayers by the Japanese government can only have deleterious effects. This is a society in which bankruptcy is necessary. But we must be careful to draw a clear distinction between this rule and the matter of guaranteeing the livelihood of the employees in bankrupted companies.

Busy Idleness

In a society where work is a virtue and idleness a vice, people will go to tremendous lengths to get to their jobs— even walking the long distance from home to office during a railway strike. Surely this is an advantage for the society. Yet such pressures can make a person uneasy and fearful of being ostracized from the communal group unless one is always busy, or at least appearing to be busy, with work, and in Japanese companies many workers simply play at being busy. What prompted Ōno Taiichi, former vice president of Toyota Motor Co., Ltd., to devise the well-known *kanban* system of inventory control was the difference between the two verbs "to work" and "to move." The two words are written with similar Chinese characters, but the character for "to work" contains the radical meaning "man" symbolizing the active role of the person. Many workers do not *work,* they simply *move.* Still, it is difficult to tell who is working and who is not. Some may be actually working one moment, but doing nothing productive the next; their days are filled with constant shifts between "working" and "moving." And all factories hire more workers than they really need, which inevitably produces surplus man/hours and workers who move more than they work. Moreover, it is not easy to identify who they are.

Ōno started out streamlining his factory by asking all workers who had no immediate work at hand to go and stand by the wall. "Don't be embarrassed," he reassured them. "It's not your fault, it's your supervisors' fault." Still, no one started toward the wall. The sense of alienation from their fellow workers that would arise if they admitted that basically they are doing nothing is so strong that they will do anything just to keep moving. Ōno then told his workers just to leave the parts they had made where they were, not to take them out of the factory. Those who needed more parts, he said, should go and get them when needed, and then to take only the amount needed each time. This is the origin of Toyota's now-famous *kanban* system, widely praised for its efficiency. Implementation of the system soon revealed that some factories were putting out excess parts; they had been delivering to other factories more parts than were needed, showing that they had surplus workers. The new system helped managers to adjust the distribution of personnel.

The problems of surplus personnel exist not only in corporations, but in government offices and other organizations as well. The trouble with the rice supply system, which is such a thorn in the government's side, may stem from a similar source. The people have failed to indicate accurately the extent of their need, resulting in ever-increasing supplies of year-old and two-year-old rice.

Rationalizing operations in Japanese companies involves not so much trying to get idle employees to work harder, but to stop the "moving" workers in their tracks. Often it is these persons, busy only with incessant movement, that are the obstacle to efficiency. The problem is endemic not only to individual corporations but to Japanese society as a whole. Japanese "move" so habitually, in fact, that we are accused of being workaholics. And yet I wonder what percentage of these people are really working? The proportion must not be large, for even in this day when declining productivity in the United States is becoming such a critical issue, it is still said to be higher than in Japan.

Unremittent Work

The third advantage of Japanese functional-cum-com-
munal groups that can become a disadvantage relates to
individuals. Once after I had given a lecture on Suzuki
Shōsan's ideas, one of my listeners posed an important
question. He was ready to accept Shōsan's role in the
development of a capitalist ethos in Japan, he said, but
there was a major oversight in Shōsan's ideas. The moment
you tell a Japanese farmer that farming is a manufacturing
industry and that he must pay attention to basic economic
principles, my questioner said, he will immediately lose
interest in farming. Japanese farmers refuse to regard
agriculture as one more economic sector to be operated
like any other industry; they literally believe that farming
is "Buddhist practice," and that cultivating the soil has a
significance that other industries lack. Because of this
belief, the man continued, they think they have license to
ignore or defy the laws of economic efficiency and to make
demands that disregard economic rationality. Told that
their attitude and practices do not conform to economic
realities, they threaten to quit farming. Something must
be done about this, he said, but what? The notion of
"agricultural labor as Buddhist practice" has become a
cancer to Japanese agriculture; it has prevented agriculture
from modernizing and rationalizing, and has made it a
burden on the whole Japanese economy.

Actually, Shōsan claimed that every occupation is Buddhist practice. The problem was that some people interpreted his ideas narrowly to mean that farming alone is
Buddhist practice. That interpretation does not faithfully
reflect Shōsan's thought; it represents a kind of exclusive
agrarianism derived from a mixture of Shōsan's ideas and

the Confucian teaching that farming is noble and commerce "unproductive."

The problem my questioner presented is a very real one, and it goes beyond the limits of agriculture in Japanese society. Japanese in general tend to find a kind of religious significance or sense of spiritual fulfillment in unremitting work, quite regardless of its economic efficiency. Indeed, many people in Japan apparently gain spiritual fulfillment even from ineffectual but incessant moving about. This tendency is particularly pronounced in agriculture where agrarianism has taken such a firm hold.

The peculiarity of this penchant among Japanese has been noted by many foreigners who have lived in close contact with them. One account was found in a diary presented to a war crimes tribunal in the Philippines, which had belonged to an American surgeon lieutenant colonel captured by the Japanese army. The author observed that when his captors grew uneasy or anxious, they suddenly went industriously to work at something, trying to regain a sense of security.

Life on the battlefront is certainly insecure, and the sense of unease must have intensified as Japanese soldiers became aware of their inevitable defeat. Rank-and-file soldiers, most of whom had come off the farms, began to cultivate gardens, claiming that rations were short; their real reason for such activity was to find spiritual relief in doing something—growing vegetables.

This sort of attitude makes it difficult to face reality and to grapple properly with the problems at hand. The mentality of those soldiers can be identified in many areas of Japanese society. People find meaning in unremitting work, even when it is totally ineffectual, and on top of that they expect their "work" to be appreciated. If their motions are not recognized as meaningful, if not productive, efforts, they are indignant and feel slighted. Because so much value is attached to the attitude of devotion to work, sometimes efforts themselves are praised more than any actual accomplishment, which, in turn, generates ever more fervent and pointless moving about.

The syndrome is chronic among members of the Japanese bureaucracy. Writer Sakaiya Taichi, formerly a Ministry of International Trade and Industry (MITI) official, once told me that in government offices, people who finish their work and leave at a reasonable hour are not regarded as particularly commendable for their efficiency, while those who stay at their desks and do the same work, drawing it out until all hours of the night, are highly esteemed for their diligence. If working overtime were simply a show of diligence put on for the sake of one's superiors, it would not present a problem. But if the worker seriously believes that overtime is in itself praiseworthy and leaving at 5:00 is shameful, this is a pathetic problem.

On the other hand, is efficiency in work always an unqualified good? This is not necessarily a self-evident matter, for in Japanese society the functional group is also a communal group, and no functional group will function properly unless it is a communal group. The only solution is to rely on the traditional ethic of self-control. Each member of the society must rigorously assess himself; he must ask himself, in his "true heart," whether what he is doing helps or hinders his community and society as a whole. If he concludes that the effect of his efforts is negative, he should change his approach; otherwise the advantages that have worked favorably for Japan will turn against him as an individual and against the nation as a whole.

Old Habits versus Immediate Needs

If, indeed, a virtue can easily become a vice, and an advantage today can become a disadvantage tomorrow, how can one control these factors? In order to make sure that your good points always work to your advantage, strict self-assessment is crucial. This applies not only to individuals but to corporations and even the nation. Only with probing self-assessment will it be clear what must be done to improve the situation. The difficult part is to do what is clearly necessary. Uesugi Yōzan made a remarkable effort to rescue his domain from ruin, but he did no more than what was obviously needed. The times were such that it required a man with unusual insight like Yōzan to perceive the obvious and exhort others to help him act on it. What Ishida Baigan preached was also self-evident. Yet both men, who insisted on rigorous frugality at a time when it should have been perfectly plain that everyone had to be frugal in order to survive, encountered tremendous resistance. The opponents of any movement to improve what is clearly a bad situation generally are blinded by habit and seek their authority in the orthodox teachings of the time—during the Tokugawa period, Confucianism and the code of the samurai class (*bushidō*); since the end of World War II, democracy.

Our nation's history shows that those who seek to overcome resistance to unmistakably necessary action must have an accurate grasp of the traditional social and psychological dynamic of the people and the ability to act on that basis. In other words, they must act on the ethic of Japanese capitalism. No matter how faithful they might be to the logic of capitalism, they will lose leadership if

173

they do not act in accord with the capitalist ethic. What our corporations and nation need most today is self-control based on the accurate perception of the Japanese tradition.

10

SHIBUSAWA EIICHI AND
HIS TIMES

In the nine preceding chapters, I have introduced the ideas
of thinkers of the premodern period of Japanese history
which, I believe, can help readers achieve an understanding
of Japanese attitudes toward enterprise and work. Some
may question the validity of my arguments. Could the
thought of the feudal Tokugawa period really be of such
significance for the Meiji period when the country was
being rapidly Westernized, much less for an age symbolized by the widespread use of computers like today? Do
these ideas not simply represent one aspect of Japanese
thought that emerged during the period of Japan's isolation from the world? Some will declare that, with regard
to the great transformation we face in this age of information, such ideas are totally a thing of the past. To demonstrate that I have not been simply contriving empty arguments, I would like to introduce in some detail the life of
Shibusawa Eiichi, whose name has arisen often in economic history.

There is a well-known phrase: "Who was the man who
built Japan's business community? If there is anyone who
could say 'It is I,' this could only be Shibusawa Eiichi."
Shibusawa was born in 1840, and was twenty-nine when

the Meiji Restoration occurred: He died in 1931 at the age of ninety-one, his life spanning the period from the feudal age, through that most turbulent period in Japanese history known as "Meiji," and on into the fourth decade of the twentieth century. Shibusawa played a major role in the economic transformation of the country, during his lifetime being connected in some way with the founding of some five-hundred companies. One of the best-known is the predecessor of the Dai-Ichi Kangyo Bank, whose total assets are among the highest of all banks in the world today. No matter how greatly Japan might change in the future, it could hardly be as radical as the transformation this great entrepreneur witnessed. He was a man who, in the words of Fukuzawa Yukichi (1834–1901), "lived two lives in one body." The traditions that were nurtured during the Tokugawa period and their relation to the future will be easier to comprehend by seeing how Shibusawa lived and why his son, Shibusawa Hideo (1892–1984), described his father's life as exemplary of the concept of "permanence and change." Shibusawa Eiichi was a figure linking tradition and modernity, and in this sense an appreciation of how he lived may help us find ways to link our contemporary age to the future.

Confucian scholar Dazai Shundai, whom I mentioned in chapter 7, urged in his *Keizairoku shūi* (Further discourses on economics) that products with high value added be manufactured in each domain as a measure to alleviate the domain's financial difficulties. Uesugi Yōzan, lord of the Yonezawa domain, began the cultivation of indigo and eventually other high-value-added products. This was around the latter half of the eighteenth century. Similar economic policies were adopted by many of the domains, and among some peasants, the old phrase "plow and eat" began to give way to a new motto, "produce high-value-added crops and sell them." As they concentrated greater effort on cultivating indigo and raising silkworms, these farmers who had been simply rice or wheat growers, became textile and dyestuff makers, or businessmen-farmers.

After Nakazawa Dōni (chapter 6), moved to Edo in 1779 and set up the Sanzensha academy, Ishida Baigan's school of popular ethics (Sekimon Shingaku) spread widely throughout the Kantō area of central Japan. Baigan's emphasis on frugality, the justness of earning a profit, and the nobility of labor served very well to support the efforts at reform being led by senior councillor Matsudaira Sadanobu, who was attempting to fortify the deteriorating state of central government finances, and the Ishida school received the unofficial support of the shogunate. Nakazawa and his followers spread Ishida Baigan's teachings along the areas bordering the great Tone River, a main trunk of transportation in central Japan at the time. The areas verging on the Tone were well suited to growing indigo and raising silkworms, as well as being close to the million potential consumers of the city of Edo. This was ideal ground for the nurturing of Baigan's teachings on the rewards of hard work, frugality, and an honest profit, and even among the peasants who did not become textile and dyestuff makers, the "make-and-sell" entrepreneurial impulse was very strong.

Shibusawa Eiichi was born on a farm that raised silkworms and produced indigo dye in this very region. The family specialized not in cultivating indigo, but in processing indigo cultivated by others into dyestuff. Thus, although they belonged to the farming class, their actual work was that of dyestuff and textile makers. The family ran what could be called a typically Japanese small business. Eiichi did not receive a formal education, but was tutored at home. His father was what I have called a businessman-farmer; he loved to study and had read many books, including the so-called Nine Classics of China. He taught his son from the age of six, but later Eiichi's tutoring was taken over by an elder cousin named Odaka Rankō. At the same time Eiichi underwent a strict training in the family business. Eiichi learned quickly and showed a precocious grasp of business, and by the time he was thirteen was already making his own purchases of raw indigo.

Reading Shibusawa Eiichi's memoirs, it is clear that his father's thinking followed that of the Ishida school of popular ethics. The rules of diligent labor and thrift were absolute, and laziness and extravagance were sinful. Through faithful observance of this way of life, the elder Shibusawa accumulated considerable capital, building the household fortune to the point where it joined the ranks of the *gōnō* class of wealthy farmers. The Shibusawa household was wealthy enough to be able to make prompt payment of amounts as large as five hundred to a thousand *ryō,* though it was still only the second most wealthy household in the village. Shibusawa's memoirs tell us that even before the Meiji Restoration, when he was a boy, there was already a "rural bourgeoisie" in Japan. In Russia, in 1906, during the last years of czarist rule, Premier Peter Stolpin (1863–1911) began to institute a series of reforms based on his belief that the modernization of Russia depended on the development of an agricultural bourgeoisie. He was assassinated, however, in 1911, by a nihilist opponent of his policies. In Japan, on the other hand, long before Perry came in 1853 to force open the country's ports, the foundations for modernization had been laid through the formation of a rural bourgeoisie under the

influence of the ideas of Suzuki Shōsan, Ishida Baigan, and
other Tokugawa period thinkers.

The year of Eiichi's birth was the year of the Opium
War in China. To witness the defeat of the mammoth
nation that Japan had viewed as the pivot of Asian civilization at the hands of the British, and watch China, unable
to rid itself of the evil opium trade, forced into semicolon-
ial status through the unequal Treaty of Nanking (1842),
was profoundly shocking to Japanese. But communication
was not as efficient as it is today, and it took quite some
time for the sense of crisis—that Japan too might fall
victim to the same fate—to penetrate through to the
peasant stratum.

In 1853, four ships under the command of Commodore
Perry appeared at Uraga; the arrival of the famous "Black
Ships" was an event that had tremendous impact on the
Japanese. Eiichi was in his teens when this tumultuous
period began. In 1859, a commercial treaty between Japan
and the United States was concluded. This treaty aroused
great indignation among many Japanese because its content differed little from the treaty that Britain had forced
on China at the end of the Opium War. Japan was forced
to agree to a variety of extraterritorial rights, forfeiting
among the most serious its tariff autonomy, so that it was
unable to impose duties of more than 5 percent on imported goods. Such conditions would make the modernization and industrialization of Japan impossible. The
United States, Germany, and the other late industrializing
countries of the time had begun their development by
protecting domestic industry through high tariff rates.
Consequently, without regaining autonomous control of
tariff rates, people reasoned, Japan could not hope to
modernize or industrialize itself. How did the Japanese

overcome this difficult obstacle to growth and advancement?

The first reaction to the situation following the opening
of the ports was to "expel the barbarians." To drive away
the alien threat, they must overthrow the government that
had agreed to a humiliating treaty, and break down the
feudal system to form a new, strong government centered
on the emperor. Once this goal was achieved, the thinking
went, it would be easy to drive out the Western powers.
Filled with the rashness of youth, Eiichi and his young
friends were inspired to plan a small-scale coup d'état.
This was in 1863, the year Abraham Lincoln issued the
proclamation freeing the slaves in the United States. Their
scheme was ultimately abandoned at the behest of Eiichi's
cautious elder cousin, but as a result Eiichi was forced to
leave his village and went to Kyoto.

Shibusawa Eiichi's talents and keen mind had been noted
by many, including some persons of samurai status. One
was Hiraoka Enshirō, a retainer of the Hitotsubashi family, which was a collateral house of the Tokugawa family
and thus very highly respected. After arriving in Kyoto,
the young Shibusawa found refuge with Hiraoka and was
eventually made a retainer of the Hitotsubashi house. It
was one of the mysteries of fate that made a farmer's son
who had once hatched a scheme to overthrow the Tokugawa shogunate into a samurai and retainer of a family at
the center of power. Shibusawa performed many tasks in
the service of the Hitotsubashi family, but perhaps the one
that displayed his talents best was the reform of the fiscal
management of the house.

In Japan at the time, it was as if the whole world of
today were crammed into its small island territory. There
were economically advanced areas, developing areas, and
backward areas. Domains like the Yonezawa fief where

Uesugi Yōzan carried out his reforms were much like backward areas where accumulated liabilities threatened early bankruptcy. The area along the banks of the Tone River in the Kantō region where Shibusawa was born was what might be called a "developing" area, and the Kamigata area, i.e., the Kyoto and Osaka vicinity, was the "advanced" area of the time. Osaka was the economic center of the country—the "kitchen and pantry of the land" (*tenka no daidokoro*)—where the rice, cotton, salt, and oil exchanges and the futures market were located; and it was there that prices for the whole country were determined. The Dōjima Rice Market, in particular, was so famous that it is said people from Chicago came to tour the grain exchange there. Accounts were settled by check, promissory note, or money order, all of which were freely circulated. The role played by banks today was taken by the Ryōgaeshō, or money changers office. Merchants deposited their cash here in exchange for a certificate of deposit that could be used for payment or against which checks would be issued. Overdrawing of accounts was possible at rates of interest between 8 and 15 percent. The Ryōgaeshō obtained loans from the Jūnin Ryōgae, a group of ten leading money changers who served the role of national bank under shogunal authorization. There was also the Okawasegumi, an organization that kept government money without interest. Johannes Hirschmeier had observed that these organizations provided the basis for the banking institutions of the Meiji period.*

Behind the development of these financial institutions was a vast accumulation of commodities and a vigorous

---

*Economic historian and author of *The Development of Japanese Business, 1600–1973* (George Allen & Unwin, Harvard University Press, 1975).

market. Some people say that Japan lacked nothing required for building a capitalist economy save the steam engine and the telegraph. Japan did not have a railroad network, but the shipping routes that extended the length of the archipelago functioned practically as efficiently. (Even today, almost half of Japan's circulation of goods consists of domestic sea transport.) Yet, though in certain respects conditions were capitalistic, the country remained at the same time truly feudal and premodern. The reason for the burgeoning capitalist economy of Osaka in feudal times was the result of an anomalous system whereby the provincial lords received tax revenues in kind, mainly in the form of rice, but were obliged to make all payments in cash. To manage under this system, the daimyo established sales agents in Osaka, called *kuramoto,* who were deputies in charge of converting domain products into cash. Accounts, in turn, were handled by brokers called *kakeya.* Hirschmeier has described the commerce of the time as unique in the world. In any case, that the economy adapted so quickly to the capitalist system following the dissolution of the feudal order was at least partially the result of the prior existence of "advanced" areas such as Osaka. Indeed, it was these merchants on whom Uesugi Yōzan had relied for support in his fiscal reconstruction plan for Yonezawa domain. Shibusawa Eiichi was in a position to learn the workings of this commercial world firsthand, and his background as the son of a textile and dyestuff maker made it easy to grasp the intricacies of the economy of the "advanced areas."

In 1866, Hitotsubashi Yoshinobu (1837–1913) became shogun. This presented Shibusawa with a real dilemma. All the while he had been acting on the principle that the Tokugawa shogunate had to be overthrown, when suddenly the conferral of the title of shogun on his immediate lord automatically made him a vassal of the Tokugawa house. Because the Hitotsubashi was one of the collateral houses qualified to provide successors to the shogunate, such an eventuality was not completely unexpected; and Shibusawa's service to the Hitotsubashi family had been justifiable inasmuch as Yoshinobu was serving the emperor more closely than the shogun in his capacities as commander of the imperial guard and defender of Osaka Bay. Yoshinobu had been well known for his political differences with the Tokugawa government. Nevertheless, serving as a retainer of the shogun was a complete betrayal of Shibusawa's principles. Just as he was thinking of resigning his retainership, an unexpected opportunity presented itself.

Napoleon III had invited Japan to participate in the Paris World Exposition of 1867, and the new shogun, Yoshinobu, dispatched a mission led by his younger brother, Tokugawa Akitake (1853–1910), and Shibusawa was ordered to join the group. Shibusawa, who had been staunchly antishogunate, had also been a determined proponent of the expulsion of all foreigners from Japan; now he would be going to Europe as a member of an official goodwill mission. But Shibusawa wrote enthusiastic reports of what he saw in Paris, which at first met with scorn among his older friends. One of them criticized him thus: "Eiichi once declared he would overthrow the Tokugawa shogunate. Then he became a retainer of the Hitotsubashi family, and now he is a devoted vassal of the Tokugawa shogunate. He once called for the expulsion of the 'barbarians', and now he mingles with them and openly professes admiration of them."

Shibusawa was not one to cling blindly to unrealistic, outmoded tenets or established "principles." Wherever he was, whether in his own home town, in Kamigata in the heart of economically advanced Japan at the time, or in Paris, he made his evaluations and judgments based on what he observed and understood of the particular circumstances in that place. His interest in and enthusiasm for what he saw in Europe was not shared by all the members of the Japanese mission; some rejected everything they witnessed.

Shibusawa's attitude is typical of most Japanese today, who are realists and pragmatists. Even a country that was not long ago an enemy may readily be considered to be worthy of respect. Japanese Communists, for example, do not hesitate to point to weakness in the communist countries. Shibusawa likewise carried with him no preconceived biases. On one occasion, aboard a French ship, he ate bread and butter and drank coffee for the first time, recording in his journal that "It was all very good." In Shibusawa Eiichi's time, most Japanese found churned butter, much more fragrant than its modern descendant, repulsive; "reeking of butter" was a common expression of disdain for things Western and foreigners in general. When coffee was introduced to Japan from Europe, some Japanese abhorrently referred to it as "soot water" or "that Islamic drink." Still, we must not forget that half a century ago most Americans felt a little nauseated at the mere sight of raw fish. Shibusawa, however, had no such prejudices against foreign foods and willingly tried them, counting some Western dishes among his favorites. In later years, in fact, he developed a preference for oatmeal for breakfast.

Tokugawa Akitake and his mission stayed in Paris for a year and a half, visiting many countries in Europe during their sojourn. In each country they were treated as guests of state, and were shown many places of interest. True, Shibusawa was amazed by much of what he saw, but not dumbfounded. He accepted the fact that the West was much more advanced than Japan without a feeling of inferiority. Guided by a banker named Flury-Hérard and a certain Colonel Wilette, the Japanese were taken to see banks and stock exchanges. Shibusawa had little difficulty understanding how they operated, and he promptly made use of his new knowledge to play the Paris stock market. He was deeply impressed by the advanced machine technology and sophisticated institutions he observed in Europe. In a letter to Odaka Rankō, he wrote the following:

> Western civilization is far more advanced than I had expected; everything I see amazes me. Maybe this is the direction in which the world is moving, a trend beyond our imagination. . . . In my view, what we must do is form closer ties with foreign countries and absorb their strengths for the benefit of Japan. This may seem to contradict what I've said in the past, but it is unthinkable for Japan to remain isolated.
>
> Prices are high here—five or six times higher than in Japan. Money circulates freely, and paper currency is used as equivalent to specie. No one country's commodity prices are free of the influence of the international market. In trade with foreign countries, Japan must adopt the gold standard; this is the only way to ensure stable prices in Japan. . . .

Shibusawa's experiences in the Osaka-Kyoto area are reflected in these words. As mentioned earlier, this area of Japan had an advanced, if rather unusual, system of finance. One of the puzzling questions of the Tokugawa period is why the shogunate did not issue paper currency despite the fact that each of the domains had its own paper currency (*hansatsu*). Even Shibusawa himself issued paper currency when he was in the process of making reforms in the finances of the Hitotsubashi family. Domain currencies were pegged to holdings in specie at reliable exchange houses and thus guaranteed for payment on demand, but the circulation of *hansatsu* was restricted to a very small area. The Osaka market operated on the silver standard, while that in Edo was based on the gold standard; exchange was conducted on a floating system of rates determined by the aforementioned Jūnin Ryōgae money changing houses. After his sojourn in Europe Shibusawa became convinced that all Japanese currency should be put on the gold standard and convertible notes, acceptable nationwide, issued; he felt the country was ready to take this step and that it could do so with little difficulty.

Shibusawa was struck by the great difference in the townscapes of his country and Europe. Familiar only with the one-or at most two-story wooden buildings that lined the streets of Osaka and Edo, he marveled at the grandeur of Paris:

> I had heard about the material wealth of Western civilization, and its wonderful machines, but when I saw these for myself I was even more surprised. The accounts that people do not pick up what has fallen in the streets and that pedestrians courteously make way for each other, are true. And the efficient means for using fire and water is wondrous; the underground of Paris is riddled with passages for fire and water! The fire is called "gas," which burns without any visible source. The flame is very clear, lighting up the night with a brightness like midday. The water in Paris bubbles forth in fountains situated all over the city, and people sprinkle the roads to keep the dust down. Citizens live in seven- or eight-story houses, usually made of stone, and more splendid than the residences of daimyo or those of nobles in Japan. European ladies are like beautiful jewels, their skin fair as snow. Even an ordinary woman would cause the famed beauties Xi-shi and Yang-gui-fei of ancient China to hide in shame. I have come to this belief after comparing European women to a few Japanese and Chinese ladies I saw at the Exhibition. . . .

He was thus impressed, yet was discerning enough to perceive that France had already reached its zenith. After listening to the speech by Napoleon III at the opening of the Exposition, Shibusawa later commented that "It was an arrogant speech, sounding as if the whole world were under his control." Having been trained in the Chinese classics from childhood, and as he always claimed, "knowing nothing of Western learning," Shibusawa was reminded by the Exposition and Napoleon's speech of the ancient Chinese poem describing how a splendid palace built by the emperor Shi Huang Di (259-210 B.C.) was stormed and burned to the ground in a battle; the poem warns that a nation is brought to ruin not by its enemies but by its own arrogance. Not long after, France suffered defeat in the Franco-Prussian War. Shibusawa later described the events of the Franco-Prussian War and World War I by paraphrasing the ancient Chinese poem: "It is France, not Germany, that destroys France; it is Germany, not the Allies, that destroys Germany."

While in Europe Shibusawa was deeply impressed by three things and thought Japan would do well to learn from them. One, although not completely unfamiliar, was joint-stock companies. In Shibusawa's hometown, which was a "semideveloped" area of Japan, it was the practice to raise funds to start a business, and when the venture bore fruit, to return the funds and a share of the profits to the investors. In those days, the silk industry in Europe was on the brink of ruin brought by the spread of pebrine disease. An effective means of fighting this parasite that attacked silkworm eggs was later discovered by Louis Pasteur, and, in the meantime, France and Italy searched the world for silkworm eggs unaffected by the disease. When trade began with Japan, they imported silkworm eggs in large quantities. Shibusawa's uncle collected funds and bought up silkworm eggs all over Japan, exporting them to Europe through the port at Yokohama. This enterprise was similar to the joint-stock companies that arose in Europe. After observing the organization and operation of stock enterprises in Europe, Shibusawa thought of a way to implement a similar system in Japan, and, on his return, set out to realize his plan. The result was Japan's first joint-stock company, the Shōhō Kaisho, opened in 1869. The company was like a combination of a general trading firm and a finance company.

Shibusawa's second important observation in Europe concerned banking. There, he noted, bankers were accorded high status in society. The two men who guided Shibusawa and his group were, as I have said, a colonel and a banker, and while, in the eyes of the Japanese, the former was equivalent to a high-ranking samurai and the latter to a merchant (belonging to what was the lowest class in Japan), the two men observed no such social distinction in their behavior toward each other. Indeed, Shibusawa saw, the colonel seemed to treat the banker with particular deference.

In Japan, even after the Meiji Restoration of 1868, a sharp distinction was maintained between government officials and all other members of society, based on the accepted "superiority" of the public over the private. Indeed, there are vestiges of this tendency in Japanese society even today. One can imagine, then, how strong in the minds of the people of Shibusawa's time were the distinctions separating the four classes of feudal times: samurai, farmer, artisan, and merchant. Shibusawa himself, who had had the rare experience of moving from the rank of farmer to that of samurai, was no doubt keenly aware of these social distinctions. It is little wonder that he was startled by the relationship between the French colonel and the banker.

A third memorable impression for Shibusawa was

formed when he met King Leopold II of Belgium. Hearing that Shibusawa's group had visited an ironworks in Liège, the king declared, "You were impressed, I believe, by what you saw there. Nations that produce great quantities of iron are without exception wealthy, and those that consume large quantities of iron are therefore strong. If Japan, too, is to become powerful, it must use iron in great quantities, and you must buy it from my country." The king was talking for all the world like a salesman! In Japan it would have been unthinkable for the emperor, or a member of the court, the shogun, or even a samurai to overtly involve themselves in matters of trade or commerce, but in Europe Shibusawa's personal belief that business could be an upright and honorable profession found confirmation.

Shibusawa and some other members of his group had planned to remain in Europe to study after their duties as part of the mission had been fulfilled, but the feudal shogunate had collapsed and been replaced by the Meiji government and they were forced to return to Japan. It was ironic that Shibusawa, once an antishogunate activist, should have heard news of the fall of the Tokugawa government while serving in Paris on a mission on behalf of that government. At the port of Yokohama, where two years previously the mission had been given a hearty sendoff, they were met by only a few friends, for they were now "enemies" of the emperor. Shibusawa immediately set out to visit the former shogun Yoshinobu, now confined at Hōdaiin temple in what is now the city of Shizuoka, to announce his return. It was there in Shizuoka that Shibusawa established his first joint-stock company, Shōhō Kaisho. Not long after his return to Japan he was summoned by the new Meiji government, which requested him to present himself at the office of the Ministry of

Popular Affairs (the Mimbushō, whose functions were later taken over by the Home and Finance ministries). When he went he found he had been officially appointed a tax bureau chief. Although he refused the offer several times, he was pressed until he felt compelled to assume the position. He served ably, eventually rising to the position of Vice Minister of Finance, in which capacity he led the implementation of many reforms. Shibusawa's insistence on balancing the national budget, however, later brought him into conflict with Ōkubo Toshimichi, a powerful Meiji government leader, and he resigned in 1873.

Tamano Seiri, a close friend of Shibusawa's at the time and chief of the Supreme Court, warned him: "It would be a great waste to resign now. You have achieved a high position in the government and have a future of great promise. Perhaps you think you will profit by leaving the government and becoming a merchant, but the world will mock you and you will be at the beck and call of government officials the rest of your life. Is that what you really want?"

Shibusawa knew that his friend meant well. The tendency to think of government officials as ranking above all others, especially merchants, was very strong at the time. But, he answered, he was not resigning for the sake of money. "Businessmen these days may be mean of spirit and not deserving of the respect of society, but this," he argued, "is not only the legacy of the feudal age; it is because merchants themselves do not conduct themselves with propriety." He related his observation that in Europe and the United States the gap between government officials and merchants was not nearly as large as in Japan, and he declared his determination "to remedy this unfortunate situation." No doubt Shibusawa was thinking of Flury-Hérard and Colonel Wilette in Paris, and he was confident that he would be a merchant who could benefit society rather than exploit it out of greed.

Soon after his resignation from public office, Shibusawa established the First National Bank (a state-operated bank that later became the Dai-Ichi Kangyo Bank), and from that time on remained active in the world of business. Though France was the first foreign country he ever visited, his greatest interest later focused on the United States. In 1879, when former U.S. president Ulysses S. Grant visited Japan, Shibusawa entertained him at his residence. Later he made several trips to the United States where he met with presidents Theodore Roosevelt, William Taft, and Woodrow Wilson. Shibusawa was convinced that close ties with the United States were of utmost importance to Japan's future.

When he reached the age of seventy, he resigned from all executive posts, and by the age of seventy-six retired completely from the business world, devoting the rest of his life to philanthropic works.

As Shibusawa Hideo recalled, his father's pronouncements in his later years seemed to clearly reflect the ideas articulated by Suzuki Shōsan and Ishida Baigan (see chapters 4–6). Hideo described his philosophy as follows:

1. Money is the by-product of work. Just as grime collects on a machine long in operation, so work produces an accumulation of money. (That is, profit is the residue of hard work.)

2. The concerns of your company are your own concerns. The company's money is the property of others. (That is, work itself should be your aim. This honesty toward an enterprise coincides with the principle of honesty taught by Ishida Baigan.)

3. Rights are invariably linked to obligations. If you give greater priority to rights than to duty, you will never gain the trust of others. (This recalls Baigan's idea that you are rightfully entitled to profits only so long as you have fulfilled your duty.)

4. Even if you are not brilliant, if you constantly strive to study and learn a business, your knowledge and experience will blossom through your work. (Think of your work as ascetic practice.)

5. Like a general store in the countryside that must stock a wide variety of goods to meet the local demand, I (Shibusawa) have had to be a jack-of-all-trades. But this was unavoidable because of circumstances at the beginning of the Meiji period. It is better for a person to learn one job and to do it well. It is no easy task to become expert in even one line of business.

Hideo also recalls: "Father also told us children, 'If I had wanted to accumulate wealth for myself and my family alone, we would have been richer than the Mitsui or Mitsubishi families. But,' and he said this with a smile, 'you must not interpret this as sour grapes!' "

Whenever anyone came to Eiichi for advice about starting a business, he always cautioned them to consider their plans in terms of four conditions:

(1) Is it morally justified?

(2) Is it a business that is in tune with the times?

(3) Is it supported by your partners?

(4) Is it an enterprise within your means and talents?

192

In addition, he stressed the importance of frugality.

Shibusawa adhered to this philosophy from his youth until his death nearly a century later. In a way this philosophy could be described as reflecting the concept of *fueki ryūkō* (lit., "permanence and change"), which the great haiku poet Matsuo Bashō (1644–94) declared was at the core of good poetry. Like the poet, who must retain an enduring poetic spirit to create verses but be ever attuned to the changing times, the businessman Shibusawa stood staunchly on the principles of conduct he saw as right, balancing them with a sensitivity to the inexorable changes occurring from one moment to the next in a century of tumult.

Shibusawa carried throughout his life something "permanent" from the Tokugawa period, for he was, after all, born and raised long before the Meiji Restoration, and would carry with him throughout his life the morals and values of that feudal age. Yet he maintained a keen sensitivity to the times that allowed him to cope with and make the best of the dramatic changes occurring both in Japan and throughout the world between the end of the Tokugawa period and the decade prior to World War II. In Osaka and in Paris, as well as in the United States, he accepted and appreciated what he found that was of virtue. He was sympathetic to the labor movement, causing irate fellow businessmen to accuse him of being a traitor. He believed in what was "permanent" or enduring, but Shibusawa saw little to be gained in attacking "change." When the present Soviet regime was established, he wrote: "There is little we can learn from the radical leftist ideals of bolshevism and communism, but I am absolutely against breaking diplomatic ties with the new government or making the Russians our enemies. They are what they are; we are what we are. It is our business to strengthen our own convictions and await Heaven's judgment. Wrong will bow to right; and the time will come when the wrong course will be corrected and altered to the right course."

Japan and the rest of the world will continue to change, but the changes we are likely to encounter can hardly be as drastic as those that shook this country during the transition from Tokugawa rule to the establishment of the new Meiji government, changes that Shibusawa Eiichi experienced directly and indirectly. His achievements in the face of such "change," I would argue, were made possible by the elements of the "permanent" in his thinking that can be traced to the thought and society of the Tokugawa period. This dynamic of permanence and change, I believe, has enduring value.

The Roots of the Modern Japanese Psyche

SOME HISTORICAL FOOTNOTES

One of Yamamoto Shichihei's greatest attributes is his facility in viewing modern Japan from a farsighted historical perspective. He has spent a great deal of time and effort going back into Japanese history to show how current Japanese mores have very deep historical roots. The following short essays were selected from many of Yamamoto's writings on this subject and have been excerpted from his new book, *Nihonjin to wa Nanika (Just What Are the Japanese?)*. In them he traces the origins of Japanese business society almost 1,000 years into the past in order to interpret modern Japan to the non-Japanese. The setting and background of the essays, rooted as they are in Japanese history, are necessarily unfamiliar to the non-Japanese. It is, however, unusual to find anyone capable of making this connection and explaining it so thoroughly. The depth of his insights well repay a reader's effort.

11

WHENCE THE ECONOMIC
ANIMAL?

I may not be the only Japanese who thought for years that "economic animal" was some kind of "beast," an embarrassingly derogatory label. One day at a lecture, however, I heard a foreign scholar tell us that there is nothing intrinsically negative about the term. Japanese have merely misunderstood its usage, he said, reminding us that we also say "political animal" without any negative connotations. His remarks impressed on me once more the sheer difficulty of language, especially when a term is transferred bodily from one language to another. The context in which "economic animal" was used in our Japanese frame of reference was always negative, so we failed to realize that it basically means no more than "a creature who engages in economic activity."

This new insight into the term made me wonder: Who might have been the first to notice the economic proclivities of the Japanese? It could not have been a Japanese, I felt sure. Looking from within our society, we have no frame of reference for discerning whether we are any more creatures of economics than other people. Only people from outside would be likely to compare what they observed in Japan with the activities in their home country and conclude that the economic activities of the Japanese were somehow remarkable. Who could it have been?

Anomaly in East Asia

My guess is that the first to notice were Korean. In 1429 a visiting Korean envoy named Park Shu-Saeng was astonished to find that anyone with money could travel comfortably without carrying his own food and supplies with him. Even before that, in 1420, another Korean named Song Hee-Kyung, visiting a Japan where farmers could get two or three harvests annually, was equally surprised to find that beggars asked for money, rather than food. Thus by the 1420s, during the reign of the shogun Ashikaga Yoshimochi (ruled 1394–1423) and his son Yoshikazu (ruled 1423–25), a money economy in Japan had spread even to beggars. There were inns where, for a fee, lodging could be obtained and horses and porters hired for overland travel. Toll ferries and bridges were also in operation.

Today this may seem perfectly normal. Yet as Professor Kim Ilgon writes,* these fifteenth-century Korean visitors had every reason to be surprised; for a money economy had yet to take root in their own country. The Yi dynasty of Korea was founded in 1392—about the time that the Ashikaga shogunate managed to restore a semblance of real, as well as symbolic, unity to Japan under the Shogun Yoshimitsu (ruled 1369–95). The decade of the 1420s, when these two Korean visitors came to Japan, came just after King Sejong had succeeded to the throne in Korea. Professor Kim cites a passage from the *Chronicles of King*

---

*Kim Ilgon, *Order and Economy in the Confucian Cultural Sphere* (Jukyo bunka-ken no chitsujo to keizai).

Sejong, describing how the Korean court imported minted coins from China in an attempt to facilitate domestic trade. Nevertheless, the Korean people continued to rely on simple barter or receipts for commodities. The coins—minted as they were from nonprecious metals—did not circulate at all.

The Korean royal court was so determined to have people use cash that an edict was issued, making it a criminal offense to carry out economic transactions without money. The first offender to be arrested for this kind of currency violation was a poor man who received a hundred lashes and was then drafted into the navy. His wife hung herself in despair, leaving behind their weeping children. So the story goes.

Professor Kim tells us further that for the first 250 years of the Yi dynasty, that is, until the late seventeenth century, the practice of money circulation did not take root in Korea. In this respect, Korea in no way lagged behind other countries in East Asia. In Vietnam, for example, money was not widely circulated until the eighteenth century. Nor was Korea indifferent to the benefits of establishing a common currency. The government did all it could to educate people in its use, but had no success. No wonder the fifteenth-century Korean visitors to Japan were surprised to find beggars asking for money instead of food.

The fact is that Japan was exceptional in the use of currency in fifteenth-century East Asia. The Korean visitors were right to think of the Japanese as a people distinguished by their economic activity—if not by their political organization. The Yi dynasty had been very successful in setting up an orderly hierarchical society and state on the Chinese model. By contrast, Japan was in the throes of political upheaval—one of those phases in its history when the forces from the lower social strata of society were in the process of overturning the old establishment. Yet currency was generally used and accepted.

Kim writes by way of explanation: "This presupposes that the overall productive capacity of society had expanded due to an increase in agricultual productivity and the societal division of labor in commerce and manufacturing. Only then can an economy emerge, based on the distribution and exchange of goods and services." Without these conditions, no government could impose a currency system by fiat, no matter how hard it might try. Conversely, once these basic economic conditions had been created, the use of currency would spread even under a weak regime without a strong central power base like the Ashikaga shogunate.

Japan had actually tried centuries earlier, in the eighth century, to institute the use of currency, but without success. Like the later Yi dynasty in Korea, the Japanese government in the eighth century was based on legal and administrative institutions modeled after Tang China. Japan first minted coins in the year 708, a fact faithfully noted in its history books; from that time until 958 a total of twelve different coins were minted under Imperial authority. (In Korea the Koryo dynasty minted iron coins in 996 and copper coins in 1102.) Over the next two and a half centuries the government tried repeatedly to get the currency into wide circulation. It was all in vain. The Emperor Ichijo ordered in 987 that the full use of currency was at least mandatory for Buddhist ceremonies such as funerals. But the effort to establish a common currency by fiat ended in failure. Instead, goods such as rice, cloth, and silk were used as media of exchange, acceptable for payment of tax revenues.

A Money Economy (Imported)

Unlike King Sejong's officials in Korea, the bureaucracy in ancient Japan was reluctant to change over to a money economy. Japanese bureaucrats were conservative—even as they are today—and the system was hard to change. Yet economic conditions had developed in Japan to the point where a common currency was needed. The government resisted the changeover to a money economy on the grounds that it would disrupt the government-fixed values pegged to commodity goods such as rice and cloth. Another excuse was that excessive minting of coins had used up available supplies of copper.

Japan was once one of the world's three great producers of copper. Almost all of the copper ore mined in Japan, however, was mixed with sulfur, and the technology needed to separate and purify the copper had not yet been developed in those times. It is not surprising, therefore, that government officials felt that the shortage of readily mintable copper was sufficient reason for not beginning large-scale coinage. Had this situation continued without remedy, the Japanese economy might have remained mired at the same stage of development for a very long time.

At this point one man, Taira no Kiyomori (1118–81), changed the tide of history. He came up with the idea of preventing such stagnation by importing Chinese currency and circulating it in Japan. The head of a powerful samurai family and a prominent figure in the court of the late twelfth century, Kiyomori overcame strong opposition from other ministers at court and approved the import of Song dynasty currency in 1164. Japan was then ripe for a money economy to develop. The imported money spread like wildfire throughout the country. The economy began growing very rapidly, creating a growing need for coins.

The results of Kiyomori's handiwork were readily apparent to the Koreans who visited Japan some 250 years later.

It is worth noting here that the samurai, though most widely known for their capabilities as warriors, were economic animals par excellence. Kiyomori was a fine example of this social stratum. He was responsible for asserting the notion of private ownership of land (as against the public, i.e., Imperial, ownership of land that prevailed under the Chinese-influenced state of the seventh century). He also led the way in establishing a money economy in Japan.

Coins imported from the Song and Ming dynasties in China served as Japan's principal currency for almost 470 years, until 1637. The fact that Japan was willing to import and make use of another country's money as its own common currency may seem very puzzling to people today. When I recounted this dimension of our history at a seminar with foreign businessmen held in Tokyo, it aroused a whole storm of questions. Perhaps my listeners had visions of the same phenomenon in a contemporary context. Assuming that Japan, for example, continues to export quantities of cars and electronic equipment to the United States in exchange for dollars, it might alternately cease printing yen and start circulating dollars as its own currency.

What did medieval Japan export to obtain Chinese currency? Gold. There was a monumental trade in gold for Chinese coins. In a detailed scholarly study of Chinese money in Japan, Mikami Ryūzō notes that China's heavy purchases of gold from Japan in those days led to a severe shortage of the money supply in China itself. The Song government had to issue large amounts of paper money to remedy the situation. If China, therefore, was the first country in the world where paper money was widely circulated, Japan was evidently responsible for that development, at least in part!

These exports of gold to China appear to be the first historical case of the kind of "concentrated overexporting" for which Japan is often criticized today. The Song dynasty fell and was replaced by the Yuan, part of the vast Mongol empire that briefly ruled much of Asia. It was the Yuan court (1271–1368) that Marco Polo visited when he journeyed to China in the late thirteenth century. In his *Travels,* Marco Polo refers to Japan as the "land of gold." His account was no doubt based on stories he heard of the gold trade just described. Accounts implying that Japan was a "land of gold" are also found in the official *History of the Song Dynasty*.

At the time China was regarded as a microcosm of the universe, where one could find almost anything under the sun. Yet, curiously enough, gold was rare there. Almost all of the gold ornaments and implements that remain from ancient times came from the states that paid tribute to China. By contrast, the gold mines in northern Japan were so famous for their productivity that they are even mentioned in the ancient Chinese dynastic histories. Those mines did not become depleted until the middle of the Tokugawa period in the eighteenth century.

In Taira no Kiyomori's day, gold was used only for Buddhist statues, gold-leafed implements, and wrought gold ornaments. It was not used for money. The way Japan traded its rare and expensive gold for massive amounts of inexpensive, foreign coins—to be used as a medium of exchange—is an excellent example of how these ancient "economic animals" would take the profitable and practical solution to a problem. Many people have pointed out that Japan could have simply minted coins using its own gold. Japan had once minted coins, starting in 708 and continuing until 958, so the technology was certainly available. Why was this not done?

Here it is important to realize that in premodern times Chinese currency was the key international medium of exchange throughout East Asia. All trade transactions between governments—e.g., if Japan wished to import something or other from Korea—could readily be settled in Chinese currency. Even if this currency was not in use among the domestic population, a government would not reject it. Japan used the expedient of selling gold for Chinese coins because gold, which was in limited use, could be traded for a very large number of coins; thus all the costs associated with the minting process could be avoided. In addition, Chinese coins were useful for international transactions.

Interestingly enough, though, Japan apparently paid for imports from China with gold dust instead of Chinese currency. Some years before Kiyomori's introduction of Chinese money, Fujiwara no Yorinaga (1120–56) presented a Chinese visitor with gold dust as a token of gratitude for a gift of some Chinese dynastic histories. This suggests that the Japanese used both Chinese currency and gold dust as mediums of exchange in international transactions. The choice was governed by expediency.

History shows that nonprecious metals were not at first readily circulated as currency, and Japan was no exception. The exchange of gold and Chinese copper coins was thus based on a kind of international gold standard.

The Money Economy: Its Threat to the Shogunate

The money economy had already begun to spread throughout the country by the time (1232) the Kamakura shogunate promulgated the first written samurai code of conduct: the *Jōei Shikimoku*. Originally consisting of fifty-one articles—supplementary articles were gradually added, ultimately totaling some nine hundred—the law pertained to the rights and duties of the shogun's direct vassals (*gokenin*) and suits involving private estates (*shōen*). It was ironic that the free flow of currency started by the samurai Taira no Kiyomori some seventy years earlier was to cause such grief to the Kamakura shogunate. For Hōjō Yasutoki, the shogunate's third regent, had promulgated the code in an effort to hold the warrior government together.

The estates of the vassals were private property. Yet if the vassals started selling them off, the shogunate would find the very foundations of its power and stability undermined. It is true that Article 48 of the Jōei Code declared it was lawful to sell a private estate, inherited from one's forebears, "out of dire necessity." Unfortunately, the very peace established under the Kamakura shogunate—ironically enough—accelerated the growth of a money economy. Estates, whose holders' fathers and grandfathers had risked their lives to acquire and protect, passed into the possession of strangers, even non-samurai, and were sold for money. Anyone with money could increase his land-holding. He did not necessarily have to display martial valor or loyalty to the shogunate. The number of "rootless" vassals who had lost their lands—their source of income—gradually increased.

How did this happen? Originally, the samurai were leading farmers, themselves owners of newly cultivated land. They were inseparably linked to their estates. Indeed, they risked their lives to defend their lands. (The origin of the Japanese expression *issho kenmei*—to strive with all one's might—is literally "to put one's life on the line for one's land.") The estate provided vassals with a means of existence. With the wide circulation of money, however, an economy unconnected to the land came into being. This gradually divorced the warrior gentry from their estates. Once the money economy was at work, the economy based on land-holding began to disintegrate at an astounding pace. This happened in other countries as well.

With its direct vassals losing their power bases right and left, the shogunate began to look very harshly at their creditors. A supplementary provision to the Jōei Code contains the following article (663):

> When loans of money are made, the wealthy profit even more through the accumulation of interest, while the impoverished suffer even greater economic pressures. Henceforth, the court will not recognize creditors' suits seeking to exact payment from a debtor. Even if he holds an official shogunal document legalizing the transaction and goes to court accusing a debtor of not paying, his case will not be taken up. Only in those cases when he has in his storehouse items taken as security for the loan will his suit be handled.

This rather arbitrary law was issued in 1297, sixty-four years after the promulgation of the original code. The word "arbitrary" is used advisedly. Although the money lending was apparently going on between vassals with the approval of the shogunate, the authorities were clearly unwilling to come to the aid of the creditor, except when proper security had been taken to back up the loan.

The shogunate's lack of sympathy for creditors was due in part to the exorbitantly high interest rates at which money was loaned. In 1226, well before the Jōei Code was promulgated, the shogunate had issued a law restricting interest rates, calling on its vassals throughout the country to observe as promptly as possible the provisions stipulated in an imperial edict issued a short time earlier. The shogunate's emphasis on three provisions of the imperial edict indicated that the dynamics of the currency economy Kiyomori had set in motion had gone out of control—even before the Jōei Code was adopted.

One of the provisions of the imperial edict taken up by the interest rate restriction law was this: "The interest from lending grain or other property (*suiko*) shall not exceed twice the original volume; the interest from lending money (*kosen*) shall not exceed the original amount." This article (17) has a long clause which contains the following passage: "In the case of loaning for one year the interest shall be 100 percent [of the principal]; even if the period of the loan extends to several years, this [100-percent-of-the-principal-a-year] interest shall not be raised." In other words, compound interest was prohibited. Obviously, if a loan with the already exorbitant interest of 100 percent per annum were to be reckoned at compound interest, it would have increased by leaps and bounds in a few years. Even with compound interest banned, debtors would have to pay several times the amount they originally borrowed within a short period. Once they borrowed any money at all, the shogun's vassals would soon find themselves in dire distress.

Mutual Savings-and-Loan Association: Pulling the Samurai Off the Land

With interest rates as high as they were, it was not surprising that people were tempted to lend out whatever idle funds they might have at hand. Seeing how easy it was to make a good profit from loans, some people naturally hit on the idea of gathering small amounts of money from a number of individuals and making it available for loans. This gave rise to a primitive form of bank known as *mujin*.

The *mujin* was actually a percursor of the modern mutual savings-and-loan association. It is mentioned in a 1255 law supplementary to the *Jōei* Code, which establishes it as Japan's oldest form of financial institution. Less than a century after Kiyomori had pushed through the import of money from China's Song dynasty, moneylending as a business had come into being, along with this early "bank."

The 1255 law includes the following article (305):

> Moneylending (*kosen*) in the Kamakura area has recently come to take the form of the mutual savings association (*mujin*). Since money is not lent without some form of collateral, borrowers pawn their clothing and other personal items. A thief knows that if he sells stolen goods his crime would immediately be detected; so he secretly pawns them to obtain cash. Even if the owner of the stolen goods discovers that they have been pawned, the moneylenders pretend not to know the name or address of the person who pawned them. This is not acceptable. Henceforward, records shall be made of the persons who pawn articles, the day the transaction took place, and so forth. If a matter is brought to trial over ownership of an item, and the moneylender fails to give the pawner's name and address, he shall be punished for stealing.

The most significant part of this passage is the mention of the *mujin-sen,* which, as distinct from moneylending, was a sort of "group financing" scheme. The leader in such a group would be a trustworthy individual who collected subscriptions from all the members and lent lump sums of money to those in need. Selection of persons to receive loans was made by bidding or a similar method. In the event borrowers should become unable to pay further subscriptions, some item(s) of their property would be taken as collateral.

The availability of funds by bidding through a *mujin* savings-and-loan group meant that even commoners could obtain land. If they succeeded in bidding for a *mujin* loan, they could purchase an estate, putting up the land as collateral and paying off the loan to the *mujin* in installments. Eventually the lands would be their own. Unlike the case of a loan among shogunal vassals, however, the ownership of such estates would be transferred to persons outside the warrior class. Wealthy moneylenders could buy up entire estates, cash on the barrelhead. Such a situation could undermine the economic foundations of the shogunate, and it could not be ignored. In 1240 the shogunate promulgated the following supplementary article (145):

> Purchase of Estates by Commoners Prohibited. The sale of private estates has been lawful as stipulated above [see article 48 of the Jōei Code introduced above], but from now on, if a private estate is sold to a commoner (*bonka no yakara*) or usurer (*kashiage*), the estate will be confiscated in accordance with recent precedents.

Article 145 and others like it were aimed at protecting the shogun's vassals; they proved less than effective, however. Those gentry (*Gokenin*) in need of money would evade the laws by keeping some of their estates in reserve, and selling or pawning the remainder but keeping it in their own name. The shogunate's hands were tied in such cases, so it added another supplementary provision (530) to the *Jōei* Code in 1284. This was as follows:

> When a vassal of the shogun sells, pawns, or presents an estate in his possession to another person, he shall continue to be liable for the *kuji* obligations to the shogunate, e.g., guard duty at Kamakura, and the new owner will serve the vassal as a follower in the performance of those obligations. The new owner shall pay a land tax commensurate with the size of the land obtained.

The shogunate recognized that estates could be sold, bought, or pawned. But no buyer was allowed to take over *kuji* responsibilities. These had to be fulfilled by the original owner of the estate. This idea was incorporated into a new law, separating public obligations from private agreements, which made the seller of the estate responsible for public duties.

Similar situations can be observed in Japan today. When you buy a piece of land from someone but that individual wishes to keep it under his or her name for some reason, then the seller must continue to pay the property tax for which the land is liable. Nowadays the buyer hands over the tax to the seller, who remits it to the tax authorities. Under the 1284 law, the buyer was directly responsible for payment of the rice tax (*nengu*) commensurate with the size of the land obtained. Obviously, what mattered most to the shogunate in peacetime was who would take responsibility for the payment of taxes.

Money as the Leveler

The Kamakura shogunate tried endlessly to cope with the spread of the money economy. The government was driven finally, in 1239, to ban the circulation of money northeast of the Kantō area. The imperial court had tried to impose a similar ban much earlier, in 1179, but currency continued to circulate as vigorously as ever. In the meantime, the structure of imperial power was overturned and the Kamakura shogunate had been founded in 1192. The ban in 1239 prohibited circulation of currency from Shirakawa, in what is now southern Fukushima, northward. Shirakawa was the checkpoint between the Kantō region and the province of Mutsu (encompassing present-day

Fukushima, Miyagi, Iwate, and Aomori prefectures). The ban (supplement 99 to the Jōei Code) goes as follows:

> Citing the precedent of a prohibition against paying taxes in silk cloth, peasants have ceased to prepare cloth for payment of land tax, preferring to pay in cash. Many articles have been added to the code year after year in an attempt to halt this illegal practice which undermines the public treasury. From now on, the circulation of money in the area from the Shirakawa checkpoint eastward [sic; northward] shall be ceased. Merchants and others who travel out [to Mutsu province] shall be prohibited from taking money with them. This restriction does not apply to travellers going toward the capital [Kamakura], however. The quality of silk cloth tendered as tax has been inferior in quality for some time. We call on you on behalf of the Shogun to order your people to return to the former practices as soon as possible, paying as they once did.

The "prohibition against paying taxes in silk cloth" mentioned at the beginning probably refers to the same law cited in the *Azuma kagami* account of the year 1226 that tells how the shogunate "issued an order today stipulating that copper coins be used instead of cloth." The order was imposed on Musashi province (now mainly Tokyo and Saitama), but the people of Mutsu used it as a pretext for paying land taxes in cash themselves.

A hundred and eighty years later in Yi dynasty Korea, King Sejong tried to stimulate the circulation of currency by banning the use of commodity goods, such as cloth and rice, and severely punishing violators. His effort was without success. In Japan, by contrast, the government tried once to ban the use of currency in 1179, and again—in the Kantō area (the present Tokyo and east)—in 1239, for it was already clear in those ancient days that Japanese preferred paying in cash rather than kind. They were very much "economic animals."

The Korean visitor Song Hee-Kyung was surprised to find beggars asking not for food but for money in 1420. Had he visited Japan in 1231, however, he would probably have remarked on the frequency of money thefts. The following order (Article 21 of the Jōei Code) was promulgated on April 20 of that year, a year before it was included in the Jōei Code:

> The intensity of punishment is dependent on the amount of stolen goods. If a person commits a minor crime of stealing between 100 and 200 *mon* in coins, he will be released on repaying double the amount. He who commits a major crime of stealing more than 300 *mon* will be exiled or confined in prison, but his wife, children and relatives, and retainers shall be allowed to stay where they live.

The Jōei Code emphasized tangible evidence, so even if a thief stole an item he would not be punished until the goods were found. If a person stole less than 200 *mon* and paid back twice that amount, he would escape punishment. The reader will have realized that the above directive contains no stipulation about penalties for repeated offenses. Commoners realized this deficiency in the law. They calculated that as long as they stole less than 200 *mon* at a time, they could repeat the crime over and over until caught. Even then, they could obtain freedom simply by paying double the money they were discovered as having stolen. It was not long before the number of thefts of less than 200 *mon* increased drastically.

Article 21 and the article that follows (263) are of interest because they show not only that money had spread even among the commoners but also how quickly a law issued by the Kamakura shogunate was felt even among the lower orders of the common people. In 1248, seventeen years after the promulgation of Article 21 above, the following supplementary law (263) appeared:

> Preserving the law established earlier some thieves, after being apprehended for a minor theft and paying it back twofold, attempt repeated minor thefts. Subsequent thefts committed will be considered the same as a theft of major proportions. [The offender] shall be handed down a punishment of exile or imprisonment. The magistrates and others who deal with the *zōnin* shall be informed of these cases.

Opinions vary about what exactly the *zōnin* were. Combining the character for "miscellaneous" and "person," the term can be defined as a servant tied to the household of an estate owner or wealthy farmer. The main job of the magistrates was to deal with troubles that arose when *nuhi* ("slaves") or *zōnin* (servants) absconded and joined another master's household. These people were at the bottom of the social scale. Thus, it is apparent that not only money but the impact of the Jōei Code filtered down to the lowest levels of society in those days.

Collapse of the Primogeniture System

Minor thefts could not bring about social reform, but the spread of money could. People's values inevitably changed. The power of the Kamakura shogunate had been based on its ability to guarantee its vassals proprietary rights to the land. That premise forced the shogunate to deal head-on with problems resulting from the spread of a money economy. The most damaging of all was the gradual disintegration of the primogeniture (*sōryō*) system, the foundation of the Kamakura government.

By the end of the twelfth century it had become common for each family estate to be divided among sons and daughters. Starting out with the small lands apportioned to them, if the children cultivated new land, they could add to the family's total property. In those days there was still a considerable amount of undeveloped land in Japan. After a few generations, the lands held by a large family might be quite extensive. The eldest son, head of the house, was responsible for the overall administration of the family estates. In case of war, the family members and their retainers made up a combat unit. The shogunate formally confirmed the eldest son's proprietary rights to the family property. In return he was obliged in times of peace to collect a land tax from the whole family and remit it to the shogunate. This was the most important of the services (*kuji*) due the shogunate during peacetime. The crux of the system was that while granting the ownership of land to individual members of the family the official Jōei Code obliged the eldest son (*sōryō*) to control all of the land.

Maintaining such control, however, soon became difficult. The house laws laid down by Hōjō Shigetoki, younger brother of the Shogun Yasutoki, includes one that states, "Even if the younger siblings (*soshi*) [are so successful as to] enter the service of the shogun, they shall not consider themselves 'independent' from the family." Here Shigetoki admonishes his children always to think of themselves as members of the family under the eldest son, not as independent warriors. The fact that he made this admonition indicates that some younger sons already sought independence. In addition, the money factor came into the picture. Having money made people more individualistic. Many refused to obey the primogeniture laws.

In time the primogeniture system became little more than a skeleton. The provincial constables (*shugo*) and estate stewards (*jitō*) appointed by the central government now held jurisdiction over each "small lord of the manor," whether an elder son or not. Court records from 1312 include a defendant's comment that "from the Tokuji era (1306–8) onward I have been independent (*kakubechi*) in accordance with regulations," indicating that the shogunate approved of the independence of younger sons in performing their *kuji* obligations. That sentence is followed by another statement, to the effect that no distinction was made between the elder and a younger sibling.

Thus the solidarity of family members and their retainers had virtually collapsed. In the mid-fourteenth century, however, their unity would be renewed in the form of kinship leagues, bound together by signed contractual agreements or pacts. These kinship leagues led, in turn, to the appearance of non-kin leagues whose members were united on the basis of signed agreements.

12

THE RISE OF NON-KIN GROUPS

During the 1987 South Korean presidential election campaign, I was surprised to learn that the way family organizations chose to vote could decisively affect the outcome. One branch of the Kim clan in Kyonsang Province, with about seven hundred members, went so far as to place an announcement in the newspapers stating that it would take a neutral stance in the election. "Clans" are inclusive lineage-based kin groups. Groups of this sort long ago ceased to exist in Japan, but they continue to be significant social and political units in Korea.

There is nothing unusual about the formation of large kinship groups in a society, as we know from anthropological studies. Nuclear family structure allows subsistence, but as a society becomes more complex and takes on functions that require the participation of many people, larger formal groups of one kind or another emerge. The most common of these are extended kin groups organized on the basis of both close and distant blood ties.

Ancient Japan is believed to have been a clan-based society. Various historical factors eroded the clans, but they persisted for some time in the form of the primogeniture (*sōryō*) system, under which family property was divided among the heirs. Thus, extended warrior families were organized under the leadership of the head of the house, who was usually the eldest son. Even this system, however, gradually broke down.

The Demise of Clans in Japan

In 1333, the Kamakura shogunate, which had controlled the country since 1192, was toppled; the last Hōjō regent, Takatoki, committed suicide; and the imperial court took power by force. These events propelled Japan into a period of political chaos that subsided only in 1392, when the unification of the Northern and Southern courts ended the rivalry between imperial contenders. The brief respite that began during the rule of the shogun Ashikaga Yoshimitsu (1369–95) lasted until 1425, when the post of shogun fell vacant for four years. Meanwhile, the ancient social order, including the primogeniture system, had collapsed altogether.

What were the reasons for the demise of the clan system in Japan? To answer this question, we must look at the factors that led to the downfall of the Kamakura shogunate in 1333.

The beginning of the end was marked by the two attempted invasions, in 1274 and 1281, by fleets sent by the Mongol Emperor Khublai Khan. Aided both times by the fortuitous occurrence of storms—called thereafter the "divine winds," or *kamikaze*—Japanese warriors were able to repulse both attacks. The shogunate had to commit all its resources to preparations, battle, and restoring stability afterward. But it had gained nothing from the war—no spoils or territory. The end result was a bankrupted treasury and war-weary citizenry.

Further, the imperial house had no intention of continuing to content itself with the figurehead role assigned to it by the shogunate. The emperors were constantly on the lookout for an opportunity to achieve political dominance. The nobility and the large Buddhist temples also retained considerable political influence. In 1323, supported by these forces, the Emperor Godaigo launched an attempt to regain power. The downfall of the Kamakura shogunate is often attributed to the extravagance, incompetence, and unpopularity of Takatoki, the last Hōjō regent. But that was not all. The direct cause of the collapse was the secret defection of Ashikaga Takauji to Godaigo's side and the attack and capture of Kamakura by one of its erstwhile generals, Nitta Yoshisada, in 1333. That assault brought the Kamakura shogunate to an end.

The forces that unleashed this upheaval had been brewed by the steady decay of the *sōryō* system, on which the power of the shogunate rested. Another factor was the spread of a money economy, the consequences of which included the creation of a class of shogunal vassals without any land. Some of them escaped to provinces far from the capital in an effort to build power bases of their own. At the same time, many of the provincial constables (*shugo*) and estate stewards (*jitō*), who were charged with administering shogunal affairs in local regions, took advantage of their positions to build up personal followings and fortunes.

In sum, Kamakura's support base had been eaten away until all it took was a single push by the Ashikaga and Nitta warlords to bring the regime tumbling down. The victory, however, did not halt the process of decline in the social and political order.

Yamamoto Shichihei

From Kin Groups to Contractual Groups

The Ashikaga shogunate was established in 1336. Like its predecessor, it was plagued by pressures from without and stresses from within. Emperor Godaigo, from a base in the mountains of Yoshino, continued his campaign against his rival in the Northern court and against the shogun. The shogunate itself was shaky, torn by internal schisms. To the *kokujin,* knightly landed gentry in the provinces, this meant that the government was not capable of guaranteeing them the proprietary rights to their land. They tried to protect themselves by making their own binding mutual commitments. This could be done only by dissolving prevailing alignments and creating new ones, which came to be called *ikki* or "compacts." Originating in China, the word *ikki* literally meant "with one goal," or "in agreement." In medieval Japan, it referred to a contractual local organization or coalition for protective or military purposes, built on personal links other than blood or feudal ties. Formed by landed warriors, merchants, and Buddhist clergy or monks, such groups appeared more and more frequently, and in the process the base of Japanese society shifted from kin groups to contractual groups.

The earliest *ikki* compactors were, in fact, family groups composed of kinsmen who united for some common cause; it was not long before influential non-kin persons were also incorporated into the groups. Gradually a variety of *ikki* compact types appeared, focused on common territorial interests. Eventually most members had no blood relations whatsoever.

Examples of the written contracts drawn up by *ikki* follow, beginning with a family compact (*ichizoku ikki*) among members of the Yamanouchi family, dated 1351:

Since the collapse of the Kamakura shogunate, this family has been entrusted with the management of these territories in return for our loyal service to the shogunal house [Ashikaga]. However, since autumn of last year, there has been discord between the two parties [Ashikaga Takauji and his brother Tadayoshi], and disturbances have erupted everywhere. Furthermore, some people take the side of the emperor [the Southern court], and others ally themselves with the shogunal house [Takauji] and Tadayoshi. The knightly genty (*Kokujin*) are divided in their opinions. The members of this family, favored with the beneficence of the military authorities, will never forget the favor shown us. Wishing to leave a legacy of military honor to our descendants, with dispatch we commit our loyalty to our *suzerain* [Tadayoshi]. We will never swerve from that determination. If hereafter any signatory to this pledge violates its terms, the case will be discussed among the signatories and an opinion will be handed down. If anyone should be false to the pledge herein, may the Brahama Deva, the Shakra Devanam Indra, the Four Heavenly Kings, all the major and minor gods of Japan, of Heaven, Earth, and Purgatory, especially those of Suwa Shrine, Hachiman Shrine, and Kibitsu Shrine of our province, mete out their punishment upon the miscreant. By this document, all the undersigned are bound to uphold this contract. So be it.

Jōwa 7 [1351], 10/7
Fujiwara no Toshikiyo (signature)
(ten other signatures)

The Yamanouchi had expanded their power as *jitō* (military estate stewards) in what is now Shōbara city in Hiroshima Prefecture. As the written pact above demonstrates, the family carried on the Kamakura-style tradition of written pledges exemplified by the shogunate's Jōei Code. The final part of the above document was very similar to the format of the Jōei Code. (Interestingly, the date reads Jōwa 7, using the era name designated by the Northern court, but that era had only six years. There was no such thing as Jōwa 7, the year 1351 being Kannō 2. The Southern court named the same year Shōhei 6. This ambiguity was deliberately contrived to signify that the Yamanouchi offered allegiance to neither the Northern nor Southern court, but only to Ashikaga Tadayoshi.)

Growing Strength of the Gentry Compacts (Kokujin Ikki)

The Yamanouchi Compact document was a simple pledge of solidarity among the eleven participants who signed it, with no other provisions. Usually there was an itemization of terms, and in some cases there were 60 or more signatories—one pact had 237! Clearly all those names did not belong to members of one family.

Ikki compacts were formed under varied circumstances, some of them extremely complex politically. In one instance, the famous warrior and *waka* poet Imagawa Ryō-shun was sent to Kyushu as the shogunal deputy with orders to subdue the powerful Shimazu family. He enrolled sixty-one southern Kyushu landlords in an *ikki*, with the purpose of mobilizing a force potent enough to take on the Shimazu.

This document, known as the "*Ikki* Compact of *Kokujin* of Higo, Satsuma, Ōsumi, and Hyūga Provinces," was headed, "*Ikki* Compact Sealed with Sacred Water." To formalize this kind of compact, two or more copies of the covenant were made; and because the pledge was considered sacred, one copy was deposited at the shrine whose deity was invoked. Another copy was burned; its ashes were mixed with water that the participants then drank in a symbolic action representing a pledge to the deity. The rite, a kind of sacred communion, bound the members together "in one mind." Under no circumstances would their vow be broken. This was a more absolute type of commitment than that of the family *ikki* pacts.

As long as the idea of family vassals loyal to a single master retained any force, there would inevitably be times when a pledge signer was caught between the competing pressures of *ikki* and family loyalty. I will discuss such cases later. Here, let us look at the 1377 agreement whose origins I have just described:

IKKI COMPACT SEALED WITH SACRED WATER
Terms of the Compact:

With one mind and of one accord we should pledge our loyalty to the great shogunal house.

(1) Now that it has been decided that Shimazu Korehisa [military governor of Satsuma] and Shimazu Ujihisa [military governor of Ōsumi] have surrendered [to shogunal deputy Imagawa Ryōshun], we should wait to hear the shogun's opinion before we destroy them or plan attacks on them. But if they, though having surrendered, should seek to take territory from the members of this compact and conflict breaks out, we should defend ourselves without shogunal approval.

(2) If a conflict occurs among any members of this agreement over their own lands, it must be discussed among all the members, and advice of the shogunal deputy be sought before a final decision is made, in accordance with the opinion of the majority and with what is right. Anyone who does not abide by this decision will be regarded as having betrayed the *ikki* compact. Withdrawal from the agreement will not be tolerated.

(3) Or, if the shogunate decrees that someone return to lands over which he originally held proprietary rights or awards new territory [in reward for services], any member who feels that his rights are violated by this award should consult with the *ikki* compact group, and only after a majority agreement is reached there, should he go to court. No member should disturb the group by reckless behavior. Complaints against the shogunate should be presented to the whole membership, appealing to right and reason.

If anyone violates these articles, may all the deities of Japan, major or minor, especially Amaterasu Ōmikami, the deity of Hachiman shrine, and the Kirishima tutelary deity of this province, inflict divine punishment on the traitor. This agreement shall be as written.

Eiwa 3 [1377], 10/28
Deputy Director of the *Daizen* Office, Tameyori (seal)
(sixty signatures)

The word *ri* (principle, reason) appears frequently in such agreements. This one, dated 1377, was written when Ashikaga Yoshimitsu was shogun. At that time the imperial house was still divided and each of the two competing branches created its own name for the era. The one used here, Eiwa, is that of the Northern court. The following year Yoshimitsu moved into his new villa at Muromachi in Kyoto, where he lived in sumptuous style, but the political control of the shogunate never reached very far into the provinces.

Yoshimitsu sent Imagawa Ryōshun to subdue by force intransigent provinces in southern Kyushu, but resistance from Shimazu Ujihisa, allied with the Southern court, led Ryōshun to organize the proprietary lords under his control into an *ikki* compact to confront the Shimazu. The above agreement was drawn up just after Shimazu's surrender. It seems that the *ikki* parties were extremely wary of the two Shimazu families whom they had just defeated. Perceiving the need to prepare for a possible counterattack and for attempts to suppress and fragment the *ikki,* the members agreed to formalize their pact and sealed it with the sacred water rite.

The reference to "conflict over their own lands" in the second article concerned individual proprietary rights over territories and the boundaries between them. The article stipulates that when disputes arose, both sides would be heard, discussion held, and approval sought by Imagawa

Ryōshun, the shogun's deputy, and decisions made by a majority following the dictates of "right and reason." If someone refused to accept that decision, he was regarded as having broken his *ikki* pledge, a very serious breach. Such conflicts were apparently so frequent that the great majority of *ikki* documents contain similar articles.

The shogunate rewarded those who were especially instrumental in handling the Shimazu affair by restoring territories that they had lost. On occasion they would award them the rights to new territories. Such awards often infringed on vested interests; the third article was meant to establish means to resolve such cases. Instead of appealing directly to the shogun or his deputy, the petitioner was supposed to present his case first to the whole pact group. This procedure, too, was set forth in most *ikki* compacts.

The Kyushu example illustrates the way the shogunate used militant local landed gentry to help suppress overly ambitious, powerful provincial constables (*shugo*) in outlying areas like the Shimazu. But because these landholder coalitions were not backed by the personal motivations of the individual landed gentry, they tended to evaporate quickly. Relying on them could be dangerous to the shogunate, and not simply because the commitment of the participants was tenuous. Forming local alliances taught the participants how to organize themselves, creating a force strong enough to oppose the constables appointed by the shogunate. Sometimes they demanded that a resident constable be replaced. When based on the shared convictions of the members, these coalitions could be very strong. An example of one written pledge, "Compact Jointly Signed by the Landed Gentry (*Kokujin*) of Aki Province," illustrates this:

ARTICLES OF SOLIDARITY OF AKI PROVINCE *KOKUJIN*
We hereby swear

(1) That if any member's land be removed from his proprietorship without due cause, he should present complaints to the whole membership;

(2) That such matters as provincial service [provincewide *ad hoc* taxes and corveé] should be brought up for discussion at opportune times;

(3) That if a situation becomes so grave as to lead to hostilities, the undersigned are to assemble without delay and decide upon measures for their self-protection;

(4) That whenever a dispute breaks out among the undersigned, the disputants will be heard by the whole membership and the problem reasonably settled.

We, the undersigned, will together obey the injunctions of the Ashikaga shogun.

If anyone should violate these terms, may all the deities of Japan, major and minor, especially those of Itsukushima shrine, visit their divine punishment on the offender. So be it as written and signed.

Ōei 11 [1404], 9/23
Shami Myōgo (signature)
(thirty-two signatures)

At first glance, this document, dated 1404, does not appear to contain anything remarkable. Yet from the shogunate's standpoint it is subversive, for it constitutes a pledge made by thirty-three landholders of Aki Province (in present-day Hiroshima Prefecture) to act together in opposition to Yamana Mitsuuji, the constable appointed the previous year.

The provincial constable (*shugo*) for Aki often served simultaneously as the shogunal deputy for Kyushu, and therefore his power was spread quite thin. The newly appointed Yamana tried to shore up his power and extend his control. Exploiting his role as an executor of shogunal instructions, he surveyed the territories of local lords within the province and rewarded those who accepted his authority with guarantees of the rights to their land. Sensing danger in such tactics, the lords of Aki formed a coalition. They most feared that their own territories would be confiscated in order to reward anyone who submitted to Yamana's control. This anxiety is expressed in the first article, "if any member's land be removed from his proprietorship without due cause . . ."

The character of this compact was completely different from the coalition of Kyushu landholders. In the former case, the compact was organized from above by Imagawa Ryōshun. The Aki lords, in contrast, organized themselves in opposition to a higher authority, the purpose of their pact being to counteract it. This was an instance of power asserting itself from below (*gekokujō*)—a familiar Japanese term.

The constable's carrot-and-stick tactic was intended as a way to divide and rule and, because of it, not all Aki lords participated in the *ikki* compact. The powerful knightly gentry under the shogunate's direct control did not join the coalition. Yamana Mitsuuji mobilized these *kokujin* gentry on his side and tried to suppress the compact. Hiraga Kōshō, the leading signatory of the pact document (under the pen name Shami Myōgo), had been at war since the previous year; his castle had been attacked, and he had lost his sons in battle. Acknowledging the clear but unacceptable prospect of being completely destroyed piecemeal by Yamana's men, he and other compact signatories agreed to join forces and fight should any of them be attacked. This was the intent of the third article, "if a situation becomes so grave . . . ," whereby they swore to defend their individual holdings jointly. In other words, an attack on one would be considered an attack on them all.

Unable to get the upper hand with the men he had, Yamana requested reinforcements from neighboring provinces. At that point the shogunate had to decide whether to send in a punitive force to assist Yamana, or to dismiss him and compromise with the *ikki* compact group. Ashikaga Yoshimitsu had retired in 1394 and his son, Yoshimochi, took the title of shogun. His father, however, continued to wield actual power. Yoshimitsu elected to compromise. Yamana Mitsuuji was sent back to Kyoto, and Yamana Tokihiro was appointed constable in his place. Hiraga and the other compact organizers submitted written vows placing themselves under the shogunal authorities, and the shogun responded by pardoning them. This brought the incident to a close. These events spanned about four years, during which time compact participants maintained a cautious stance. By including a fifth article that stated, "We do not oppose the shogun, but defy the constable who has abused his authority . . . ," they left the door open for compromise.

The formalizing of the *ikki* compact amounted to victory. Thereafter the constable could no longer ignore the wishes of the gentry but had to find ways to compromise with them. The participants in the pact nevertheless perceived the need to remain on their guard. They could not disperse even after the shogunate's intervention, for left on their own they would topple like tenpins in an attack. So the compact was perpetuated, eventually becoming something of a local institution.

Absolutist Compact and the End of the Sōryō System

Other *ikki* compacts that were formed during the same period put up opposition that led to all-out battles. One such struggle was provoked by Ogasawara Nagahide, appointed as governor of Shinano Province (the present-day Nagano Prefecture). At first, wishing to assert authority over all the provincial domains, he naturally refused to recognize the gentry's control over privately administered lands. His efforts produced active resistance by landholders all over Shinano that turned into a general uprising. The two sides fought it out, the constable was routed, and he retreated to Kyoto. Ogasawara's failure, occurring as it did during the rule of Yoshimitsu, when the Ashikaga shogunate was at its strongest, symbolized the failure of the shogunate ever to extend firm control throughout the provinces. Gradually the compact leaders secured real power and the shogunate's authority was reduced to nominal jurisdiction. This process led Japan into the Sengoku, or "warring states [i.e., domains]," period (1467–1568).

But *ikki* compacts of this sort were also not altogether secure. One source of tension was the incompatibility of feudal loyalties and *ikki* commitments. In family *ikki*, this problem did not occur, for the two kinds of obligation overlapped. But we can see the emergence of stress in the gentry pacts. In the Aki incident, for example, the *ikki* leaders included members of the powerful Mōri family, but not all the Mōri joined in the pact. Such situations could divide families and pit members against each other in battle, some fighting on the side of the *ikki* compact people and others on the side of the constable. There are, in fact, *ikki* compacts containing articles intended to avoid just such an outcome.

Egalitarianism and Collectivism

What motivated the formation of this kind of society? The prototypical warrior family was descended from men who cleared and settled new land, depending on their own resources. Such people had to be self-reliant and autonomous. Naturally there were areas of common endeavor, but participation was a matter of individual choice, and all men who joined in did so on an equal footing. The members of an *ikki* compact organization were all equal; as a rule, they all took part in preparing the compact draft and they individually decided to abide by its terms. Only then could a compact be set up.

This procedure became the foundation for egalitarianism and collectivism in Japanese society, for collectivism cannot be sustained without equality among members. Structurally, the concept took the form of group deliberation that operated exactly like a round-table discussion. And it was precisely in this form that the participants signed their names: The names were written radiating out from a hub, a method that removed any implications of rank. This practice is what is known as the *kasa-renpan*, or "umbrella joint signature." An *ikki* pact needed leaders, but they were supposed to be no more than *primus inter pares*, first among equals.

The main question here is how far concepts of self-reliance, individualism, and collectivism penetrated throughout society. The practice of debating and making decisions according to the majority, based on severance of kinship ties, individual units, judgments by "justice and reason," first appeared in large temples like Enryakuji and Kōyasan, under the influence of the idea that priests, who had left secular society, were supposed to be equal before Buddha. The Kamakura shogunate adopted a similar method when it adopted the *Jōei* Code through majority voting based on "reason" and free of kinship ties.

This influence spread to the small proprietary lords in the provinces in the form of sentry compacts, and from there to the peasants, who turned to the *ikki* compact as a means of collective opposition to provincial landholders. Records of events and other evidence strongly suggest that such activities among peasants began quite early, but I have never seen a peasant coalition document from the late Kamakura or Ashikaga periods. It is likely that at the time most of the agreements were made orally.

It is certain, however, that by the beginning of the seventeenth century, when the Tokugawa shogunate was established, peasant *ikki* compacts had become common. The most telling evidence lies in the prohibition order against *ikki* that was promulgated throughout the country. It read: "To form conspiracies, inscribe pledges, or take vows with sacred water of binding solidarity is forbidden by the shogunate. Anyone who commits those acts, even for a just cause, is to be punished." The prohibition did not put an end to the *ikki* compact, however. Indeed, the Tokugawa period is sometimes known as the "era of peasant uprisings," for peasant uprisings are what people think of today when they hear the word *ikki*. It is probably safe to say that peasant *ikki* developed in tandem with those of the landholders. The values of self-reliance, egalitarianism, collectivism, and performance of ability would effect lasting change in Japanese society, removing the base of kin relations, and we can probably trace the origins of this change to the Ashikaga (or Muromachi) period (1338–1573).

Ikki Compacts and Contemporary Japan

Whether one speaks of East or West and whatever term is used, the idea of medieval "peasants" usually evokes images of serfs bound to the land. Some might strongly object to the assertion that Japan never had slaves or serfs. The supplementary articles to the Jōei Code indicate that traffic in humans did take place, and the laws regarding the treatment of slaves (*nuhi*) and servants (*zōnin*) imply that some did indeed live in virtual bondage. This granted, however, medieval Japan never had public slave markets or put up slaves for auction, nor was there a recognized hereditary slave caste. In other words, slave- or serf-holding systems never became social institutions recognized by law. To understand why this should be so, let us look first at Article 42 of the Jōei Code:

> In various provinces, when a peasant flees the land, his master sometimes holds [the peasant's] wife and children and seizes his property, calling these "booty" (*nigekobochi*). Such an act runs counter to benevolent government. If court judgment determines that the peasant has left some amount of his land tax unpaid, the part of his property that would make up for the amount should be seized. Nothing more should be taken. Whether to depart or remain is to be left to the will of the person.

The end of the article has always been problematic in interpreting the status of peasants of this period. Its statement that it was up to the individual whether to stay or leave amounted to recognition of the right of peasants to abandon their land if they wished. If the law recognized the right of desertion, in no way could the medieval peasant's situation be construed as serfdom or slavery. In a slave society the owner has the right to hunt down escaped slaves and have them returned. The single major Western source that rejected this principle is the Old Testament book of laws, Deuteronomy. In light of this, the Jōei Code is quite remarkable, and there is as yet no definitive explanation of its social genesis.

Unmistakable evidence that human beings were actually

bought and sold can be found in the Jōei Code's supplementary Article 309, which forbids "abduction of humans
and sale of humans," and later uses the term "trafficker in
humans." The Kamakura shogunate, in fact, was troubled
by the existence of such practices among the direct shogunal vassals. But laws prohibiting commerce in humans
were well established, appearing even in the eighth-century
Ritsuryō Code.

Laws such as the Jōei Code that confirmed peasants'
freedom to move about were one side-effect of the short
supply of labor in the feudal period. Fleeing peasants were
welcomed, particularly in outlying areas, and some places
so badly needed labor that they even purchased it with
money.

The tendency to welcome and assist peasants escaping
their circumstances continued through the beginning of
the Tokugawa period in the seventeenth century. In Kaga
domain (today's Ishikawa Prefecture), facilities were even
set up expressly to accommodate such peasants. I cannot·
help wondering if the statement, "Whether to depart or
remain is to be left to the will of the person," was a
deliberate stipulation that the shogunate could use to refuse to accept petitions for redress from powerful temples
and noble houses if peasants fled from their estates to those
of warrior houses.

Roman law and American law until 1866 recognized
slaves as personal property and sanctioned the apprehen-
sion and return of escaped slaves. There was no such law
in the Jōei Code. Not only were slaves protected by the
provisions noted above, it was also clear that if dissatisfied
peasants suddenly decided to leave, estate management
would be in a shambles. Article 41 of the Jōei Code,
moreover, provided that if anyone, even the lowliest of
servants, deserted to another estate, after a ten-year period

his or her new status would be legally recognized "with no question of right or wrong." As various problems arose, the laws were revised with supplementary articles, but these did not put an end to peasant defections.

The shogunate may have secretly applauded when peasants left the huge temples or noble estates for the estate of a warrior house, but there could be trouble if they went from one small landholding to another, and members of landholders' *ikki* sometimes drew up agreements promising to return each other's peasants. The *ikki* compact of the Matsurra Faction, for example, says: "Regarding peasant deserters: If there is an appeal from a private landholder, there will be no discussion and the peasant will be returned."

As relatively free members of society, peasants could form *ikki* coalitions of their own. The decisions they made were made together, through discussion among equals, and this procedure became part of the social tool kit for all Japanese. Finally, it led to the dissolution of kin groups and the shift to contractual groups as the base for social organization. In this way, *ikki* helped lay the foundations for modern Japan.

13

FORERUNNERS OF JAPAN'S MODERN THINKING

"Japanese are not very specific about things. They talk in ambiguities. Is that because Japan has never had freedom of speech?"

"Not at all. Japan has had more freedom of speech than Europe has had. Japan had nothing like the trial of Galileo or the 'monkey trial' about evolution. No Japanese Giordano Bruno was ever burned at the stake for atheism. Calvin didn't burn Servetus at the stake in Japan."

"True enough. But wasn't that because the Japanese had no Copernican theory, no idea of evolution, no atheism?"

"No, we had them all."

This question-and-answer exchange took place during a lecture I was giving to foreign businessmen residing in Japan on "Japanese Thought and Behavior." The questions took me by surprise. When I came back after the coffee break and saw the faces in the audience still registering disbelief, I wondered how this basic communication gap could ever be bridged.

It is true that "freedom of speech," as an abstract concept, did not exist in Japan. In practice, however, Japan had far greater freedom of speech than Europe had, although we had much the same diversity of theories and beliefs. In fact, my questioners had opened a very important line of inquiry for understanding contemporary Japanese thinking.

Tolerance in Premodern Japan

It would not be entirely correct to say that Japan in the Tokugawa era (1603–1867) had freedom of speech; it was not really a concept at issue. What we had was "noninterference." Indeed, in comparison with Western Europe, where heresy was not permitted and severely punished, there was a remarkable degree of noninterference when it came to the thought or religious beliefs of the common people, particularly the townspeople. One reason for this was that it hardly mattered what they thought or believed. The samurai ruling class retained the prerogative of cutting down on the spot any commoner whose behavior or speech might go too far, that is, threaten the government or the social order it sponsored. The military authorities of the shogunate were basically disdainful of the townspeople and indifferent to what they said.

Another reason for their noninterference policy was the absence of any absolute religious authority. Three major systems of religious thought coexisted in the daily lives of the people—Buddhism, Shinto, and Confucianism. The Confucian scholars of Mito were free to curse and condemn Buddhist doctrine. They might even attack the memory of Prince Shōtoku (574–622), a devout promoter of Buddhism. The Nativist scholars (*Kokugaku*) could subject Buddhism or Confucianism to the bitterest criticism. The Buddhists might rebut all such attacks with equal ferocity. Yet as long as their rivalry did not disturb the peace or erupt in violence or rebellion, the shogunate was content to leave them alone.

Of course there was no Pope, no Inquisition, and no heresy trials; the Tokugawa shogunate ran a very pragmatic, nonideological regime, working within the context of these three systems of thought. It is true that Christianity had been outlawed (largely for political reasons). But Western learning as such was not banned. A leading thinker such as Honda Toshiaki (1744–1821) might praise Christianity and Christian society. If he did not go beyond the bounds of theory, the Tokugawa leaders had no reason to silence him.

In this peculiar environment of "free speech," it was not surprising that an astonishing array of intellectual speculation and inquiry should have flourished. It is impossible here to discuss even briefly all the thinkers of Confucian, Buddhist, Nativist, or Western learning or the scholars who developed *wasan* (Japanese mathematics), agronomy, or the many other original philosophies that emerged. I would like, rather, to limit my discussion by introducing only those thinkers who made contributions to East Asian thought original to Japan—whose ideas form the undercurrent of Japanese thinking continuing into the late Tokugawa era (nineteenth century), through the turn of the century, and into the modern prewar and postwar periods. Because even then I could not do justice to the large body of learning that exists, I shall choose certain representative persons of like thinking as the next-best alternative to a more comprehensive treatment. Tokugawa thought reflected, after all, the legacy of previous centuries of intellectual inquiry and insight. Thus the wealth and diversity it displayed is unavoidably large. We can assume that it significantly shaped basic Japanese thinking in subsequent times.

Tominaga Nakamoto's Idea of Accretion

In 1726, in the thriving merchant city of Osaka, the Tokugawa government approved the establishment of a private academy called the Kaitokudō. As long as Osaka's wealthy townspeople wished to put forth the funds to educate their children and young persons in their employ, the shogunate was happy to lend its encouragment and its stamp of approval. Having obtained this official approval, the academy was inevitably subject to whatever ideological censorship the shogunate might deem appropriate. The townspeople knew this, but did not object. From all outward appearances the Kaitokudō was an academy that taught Zhu Xi (Chu-Hsi) neo-Confucianism, the orthodox school of thought of the shogunate. But it was, after all, set up and run by townspeople. Their "merchant's logic" was bound to set the tone of its schooling. Whatever did not suit Osaka's pragmatic mind-set was likely to be put quietly and politely aside.

The Kaitokudō was built on land provided by the Dōmyōjiya, a soy sauce maker who was one of the five powerful townsmen who founded the school. The third son of the soy sauce maker was Tominaga Nakamoto (1715–46), who showed unusual genius from an early age. He is one of the scholars I would like to introduce here. First, let us take a look at the academic style of the Kaitokudō, where Tominaga and Yamagata Bantō, whom I shall also discuss, began their studies. The Kaitokudō, like the Shingaku Kōsha academy run by Ishida Baigan (1685–1744) and others, was a townspeople's school. But its atmosphere was quite different from the others. Ishida's school of popular ethics (*seikmon shingaku*) might be described in contemporary terms as oriented to the small enterprises that concentrate diligently and determinedly on a modest scale of business. By contrast, the Kaitokudō catered to the "big business" of the city. Once these merchant houses had achieved a position of stable prosperity, their leaders began to turn their attention to satisfying their intellectual curiosity rather than to expanding their businesses further. The Kaitokudō remained open until 1869, the year after the Meiji Restoration.

Business was the townspeople's foremost concern. Learning, therefore, was not the pure contemplation of the ascetic priest; nor was it, in the Confucian tradition, the effort to seek entrance into the innermost circle of a respected teacher's disciples, devoting oneself entirely to Confucian learning. Work came first. One of the Kaitokudō school regulations states:

> Learning is for the sake of practicing loyalty and filial piety, in pursuit of one's vocation. Lectures are aimed only to encourage these pursuits. Even those people who do not have textbooks with them may come in and listen. They may leave midway in the lecture, if they have important matters to attend to.

With rules like that, the school must have had a considerably liberal character.

Impracticality, obviously, went against the logic of the merchant. The shogunate advised that the school should teach only the Four Books and the Five Classics of Confucianism, as well as moral instruction; but this did not work out in practice. All kinds of people came to the school, which offered lectures from many schools of thought. Viewed critically, the Kaitokudō offered merely an academic hodegpodge, or, seen positively, a richly varied menu of progressive learning. But the students were not put in a position where they had to accept what the teachers said as absolute. They were free to disagree with

any lecturer or teacher they heard. Of course, no certifi-
cates or qualifications were to be obtained by studying
there. It was a school in the true sense of the term.
Tominaga Nakamoto's thought had its beginnings in this
very free atmosphere at the Kaitokudō.

Let me now explain the crux of Tominaga's thought, as
discussed in his two major works, *Shutsujō kōgo* (Comments after meditation) (1744) and *Okina no fumi* (Writings
of an old man) (1738). Read in the original, these books
are very difficult for us moderns. Buddhist scriptures are
frequently cited and there is abundant use of Buddhist
terms, not to mention an archaic style of writing. At the
beginning of the *Shutsujō kōgo,* Tominaga says:

> Studying the times during which Buddhism began, [I conclude]
> that it originated in various schools of thought. There were about
> ninety-six of them, each viewing Heaven as the ideal world. What
> they taught would boil down to this: "If you discipline yourself
> you will be reborn in Heaven."

Tominaga then goes on to declare that the existing Buddhist scriptures were not the words of Shakyamuni, but
the creations and additions of later personages who used
his name to give authority to their own assertions. Such
accretions Tominaga calls *kajō*—a key word in his thought.
He uses the term for the first time in the following passage:
"[the notion of] the 'six worlds'—such as those of empti-
ness, materialism, and greed—is the product of mutual
accretion, so the content [of these concepts] is nebulous,
and it is impossible to tell whether they are authentic."

What Tominaga was saying would have been tantamount
to heresy in the context of Christianity. It was as if a
believer in the Bible as Holy Writ were to claim, for

example, that "The Second Epistle of St. Peter in the New Testament was not written by St. Peter." What would have happened in Europe in the mid-eighteenth century—when the above books by Tominaga appeared—if someone had declared: "Those words were believed to have been spoken by Christ. Actually they were just a collection of citations from the Old Testament, teachings from Judaism, and phrases created by people at a later date and attributed to Christ to give them authority. In the end the Bible is merely a collection of notes by those who compiled it." Even today this assertion would be rejected and attacked by fundamentalists, inasmuch as they believe the Bible is the word of God.

Thus Tominaga's concept of "accretion" meant additions to the words of someone who possessed absolute authority, in order to give them legitimacy. Today it is not unusual to analyze religious scriptures the way Tominaga did. Computers have even been mobilized for that purpose. However, in the world of Western European Christianity such analysis did not begin until after the turn of the twentieth century and was not acceptable until after the end of World War II. Even now fundamentalists virulently oppose such interpretations. Biblical scholars often come under severe attack as agents of Satan, and are still not completely free to study as they wish.

What would happen in the Islamic world—in Saudi Arabia or in Iran since the time of Khomeini—if you were to say "The Koran is the sum of the miscellaneous teachings of different religions, and such and such a passage is a citation from . . . "? You might be even more severely denounced than was Salman Rushdie for his controversial book *The Satanic Verses* (1989)—and no doubt sentenced to death.

Nativists Applaud Tominaga

There were probably few places in the world during that first half of the eighteenth century when Tominaga lived where a person could say with impunity that a sacred book did not represent the words of the sage to whom it had long been attributed. Tominaga was a man of unusual genius, and the Japan that produced him was truly unique. No doubt the stage was set for such a thinker by the coexistence of Shinto, Buddhism, and Confucianism. Tominaga's theory naturally encountered fierce resistance from Buddhist scholars, but it was highly applauded by Motoori Norinaga (1730–1801) and others of the nativist school of learning.

The rebuttal from Buddhists was searing, but Motoori was not moved. Commenting on the priest Musō in a book attacking Tominaga, he wrote:

> [The priest] is upset because he thinks the Way he has been pursuing was treated lightly. His discourse, however, is only strident emotionalism, and there is not one passage that presents a convincing counterargument. What a shame that even a priest like Musō, who has diligently studied Buddhism, cannot present a cogent refutation of Tominaga's work.

The priest's indignation was probably all the greater to think that an upstart, the third son of a soy sauce maker, should have the impertinence to say that the sutras were not the teachings of Shakyamuni. It was tantamount to denying the truth of the words "I heard my teacher say," as stated by Shakyamuni's disciples in the Buddhist scriptures.

Tominaga's *Shutsujō kōgo* was also taken up by Hirata Atsutane (1776–1843), who considered himself a disciple of Motoori. Hirata apparently took advantage of the book in order to negate Buddhism, writing:

> [Tominaga] read many books on Buddhism, and with unusual insight he perused all the scriptures of the Buddhist Law and came up with the enlightening theory that even the greatest priests, long revered as founders of sects in the country where Shakyamuni was born, had never directly heard or read his words. The theory holds that none of the Buddhist scriptures were direct teachings of Shakyamuni. They were all fakes of a later period, he discovered.

Hirata went a bit too far when he said "fakes." Tominaga said they were accretions, but not out-and-out "fakes." If the Buddhist scriptures were fake, then the teachings of Confucius and the legends of the Shinto gods would be fakes as well.

Indeed, Tominaga went on to apply his theory of accretions to Confucianism and Shinto in his next book *Okina no fumi*. He states:

> The reason that Confucius preached the rule of right by expounding the teachings of the ancient sage kings Yao and Shun, and of the Chou dynasty kings of Wen and Wu was because he wanted an alternative to the rule of force practiced by the Qi dynasty king of Huan and the Jin dynasty king of Wen. . . . Confucianism itself was divided into several different schools. They show how [his disciples] utilized the teachings of Confucius in their own way, adding their interpretations.
>
> The same is true of Shinto. People in ancient times put forth their interpretations of ancient practices and legends and called them the "Way of Japan" to outdo the teachings of Confucianism and Buddhism . . . Buddhist and Confucian teachings are all international additions by people of later generations. Shinto, likewise, is not the way things were in the age of gods. . . .

If Hirata, an advocate of the "ancient way" (*kodō*) and the revival of Shinto, were to praise Tominaga's theories in order to put down Buddhism, then he would also have to admit that the old writings about the Shinto gods were fakes. From the point of view Hirata took, it would have to follow that Tominaga had renounced Shinto, Confucianism, and Buddhism. But we can consider his method similar to the textual criticism of Biblical scholars, as an exercise in understanding the history of textual compilation. We may say that he studied Buddhist scriptures, Confucian texts, and Shinto legends, not as the writings of absolute truth based on faith but as objects of scientific analysis.

How did Tominaga proceed to this understanding of the Buddhist scriptures, which are far larger in number and far more complex than the Bible? His approach was basically the same as modern methodology. We may conclude this from the writing of Mizuta Norihisa, a specialist in Tokugawa thought, in his study of Tominaga:

> Tominaga Nakamoto determined chronological order in the development of thought by looking at the the nature of its content, the intensity of the nostalgia for antiquity, and the degree of exclusivism—all reflecting the inevitable mind-set of those who create arguments to overwhelm others. The fact that his attention was directed this way might seem a matter of course at first glance; but these were truly ingenious yardsticks, of very high probability. Having viewed intellectual in reverse chronological order, Tominaga then shed light on the developmental process in chronological order. While considering various problems that occurred in this process, he reorganized without prejudice aspects of the historical development in a given text. This method, close in its way to modern textual criticism, is a sure and fundamental method of study in intellectual history.

Modernity and Originality

In explaining his principle of accretion, Tominaga postulates three conditions of language that shape the development of ideas: (1) people (sectionalism); (2) time (historical context); and (3) type (diversity of usage). He begins his discussion by observing that the *"Hannya shingyō* ("Heart Sutra") does not include the term *busshō* (Buddhanature), and the *Agon* Sutra does not use the term *dharani* (mystic Buddhist incantation). . . ."

Modern examples could be cited for all three: (1) Christians do not use the term *jōbutsu* (attaining Buddhahood); (2) the Tokugawa era did not have the term socialism; and (3) the *kami* (Japanese deities) are not the same as God.

Tominaga did not think that accretion and the three conditions were the only principles that could universally determine the language of thought. He claimed that thought in each language is formed by the three conditions. From this point of view, the notion of "universal human thought of eternal validity" is from the outset a fiction. No doubt Tominaga would have seen the twentieth century, when believers in such fictions fought world wars at the cost of tens of thousands of lives, as an absurd century of retrogression.

He postulated five "type" conditions. His classification is not completely explicit, and there are several theories as to how to interpret it. The five types, as interpreted by Mizuta Norihisa, are as follows: (1) extensive, abstractive, metaphorical usage; (2) undeveloped, general, universal usage; (3) explosive, deepening, thorough usage; (4) antonymous, reverse, antithetical usage; and (5) inferential, deductive, revolutionary usage. It would be interesting to study how terms like "peace" and "people" are used in different countries in accordance with Tominaga's classification. Nevertheless, his explanation of the above classifications is not as clear as the three conditions. Probably he did not have enough time to expound his ideas thoroughly, as his early death approached.

Tominaga thought that the tendencies determining accretion varied from one folk culture to another. In other
words, he introduced "cultural type" in addition to the
above principles, anticipating the perspective of cultural
anthropology.

This idea is discussed in *Okina no fumi*. Tominaga calls
the tendencies "cultural proclivities." He writes, "Buddhism, Confucianism, and Shinto each have their own
unhealthy peculiarities in teaching. The follower must be
careful not to be fooled." He says that the peculiarity of
Buddhism is "magic," that of Confucianism is "rhetoric,"
and that of Shinto "mystique, secrecy, and initiation."
The process of accretion amplifies those proclivities and
makes them intractable. Introducing the proclivities of
Buddhism or Confucianism from other cultures is pointless, Tominaga says. The Japanese attachment to transmis-
sion of secrets (as a kind of initiation) is "deplorable," he
says. He warns that it is not a "way of truth" to transmit
to only a few what is arbitrarily set up as valuable.

Considering how original and modern Tominaga's
methodology was, we cannot but be impressed with his
genius. Tominaga was a truly outstanding figure in human
history. In Western Europe it was not until the twentieth
century that a scientific method similar to Tominaga's was
devised to analyze the Bible, which demonstrated, among
other things, that the Five Books of Moses were not
Moses's writings but a product of accretion.

What kinds of norms did he think his countrymen
should have when he said, "Buddhism is the way of India,
Confucianism the way of China. They are foreign ways,
not Japan's. Shinto was the way of Japan, but only in the
past, not now"? He was not, of course, an advocate of
anomie. He says:

Do what you are supposed to do. Work hard, be honest, behave
well. . . . If you have a master, try your best to serve him. If you
have children, teach them well. If you have vassals, control them
well. If you have a husband, follow him faithfully. . . . Stay where
you live, follow the customs, and observe laws and regulations.
. . . These are only natural things to do, in accordance with the
principle of the universe. You do not have to turn to Buddhism or
Confucianism to know that.

In other words, rather than renouncing Buddhism, Confucianism, and Shinto, Tominaga tries to provide his own
accretions to the three. In short, he taught a secular moral
code and "situational ethics." In 1966, the American the-
ologian Joseph Fletcher published a book entitled *Situational Ethics: The New Morality*. The Western countries
where Christianity prevails tend to have firmly fixed
ethics, and they have always expressed principles as universal human principles. Tominaga would describe this as the
proclivity of the Christian countries of North America and
Europe. This, of course, does not mean that he and
Fletcher share the same ideas. But Fletcher quotes a passage from Alfred North Whitehead at the beginning of his
book—"The simpleminded use of the notions 'right or
wrong' is one of the chief obstacles to the progress of
understanding"—which reminds us of Tominaga. In Japan
today there is probably no one who disapproves of his
ideas. Of course I exclude those who have given in to
ideological hypocrisy.

Each time I see honest and diligent Japanese say "*Watashi
wa mushūkyō desu*" ("I have no religion"; "I do not belong
to any particular religious sect"), I recall Tominaga. It is
too bad that he died so young. Even as he enunciated the
concept of accretion, he no doubt considered his own ideas
as accretion to the accumulated thought of past generations, and recognized that further accretions would be
applied to his ideas in the future.

One cannot help wondering about the intellectual heritage that led to Tominaga's ideas. We cannot attribute them simply to the environment in which three religions (Buddhism, Confucianism, and Shinto) coexisted. There are many studies dealing with this question (and no space to pursue them here). Suffice it to say, in closing this brief look at the ideas of Tominaga, that he is a figure who disproves the often-heard theory that Japanese are lacking in true originality.

Merchant Scholar

Yamagata Bantō (1748–1821) was another Edo-period thinker, also a product of the Kaitokudō, who demonstrates the "modernity" of Japanese thought. He was born two years after Tominaga died at the age of thirty-one. By this time, the status and lifestyle of the townspeople had improved considerably in Tokugawa society. The Kaitokudō school had a history of twenty-two years. When Yamagata entered it, it had ceased to be a hot-bed of miscellaneous learning. The quality of teaching had improved, and the school had acquired a well-established reputation.

The school rules had been revised. At the time of its foundation, one of the rules had been that samurai were to be given preference in seating. This was later changed: "Students, high and low, rich and poor alike, shall be equal, except that there shall be a distinction between adults and children, and that a better seat shall be given to students enrolled at the school earlier, to older persons, or to persons of superior learning." The Kaitokudō had ceased to sanction the privileges of the samurai and discrimination in terms of social rank or wealth. The new rule reflected the greater self-confidence of the townspeople and their rising social status.

Another major change was the shogunate's approval of lectures using poetry collections and medical books. These changes are evident in the differences between Tominaga's and Yamagata's thinking. The former knew nothing of Western Europe, and his ideas showed no sign of Western influence. In the work of Yamagata, however, we can detect the influence of Western studies, from Copernicus to Newton. This was because the school had started giving lectures on medicine. Inevitably, medical and other sciences of the West began to be taught, together with Zhu Xi neo-Confucianism. Whether the sciences were Western or Oriental, the Kaitokudō's emphasis was on practical learning based on the logic and pragmatism of the townspeople. Thus, at the time Yamagata began attending its classes, the school offered a higher-quality, broader-ranging, more comprehensive education than in earlier days.

Whereas Tominaga was a son of the owner-head of a large soy sauce maker, Yamagata was the senior clerk of a merchant house, Masuya, which traded in rice and lent money to *daimyo*. Once on the verge of bankruptcy, Yamagata had rescued the Masuya and had made it into a strong funding source for several dozen *daimyo* in different parts of the country. Displaying outstanding managerial expertise, he was instrumental in the successful restoration of the fortunes of the Sendai and Oka domains. He was what we call today a "hired president."

In the latter part of the Tokugawa era in which Yamagata lived, many domains suffered from dire financial difficulties. Some were placed under the management of large urban financiers or factors. One of these powerful townspeople, the head of Masuya, was an influential member of the Kaitokudō. This was probably how Yamagata began studying at the school. When he first entered is not known.

Yamagata Bantō's real name was Hasegawa Kyūbei. The meaning of the name Bantō, his scholarly name (*gō*), is a matter of dispute among researchers, but the most reason-able interpretation is that it echoed the word for "senior clerk" (*bantō*), although the characters are different. Ya-magata was the family name of Bantō's master (the owner of the Masuya), which meant that Bantō was treated as a member of the family after his success in reviving the fortunes of the business. Able manager though he was, Bantō was after all the clerk of the Masuya firm. The huge number of books he read were all purchased by the Ma-suya, it is said. Apparently the Masuya rewarded his achievements in business by sparing no expense in buying him books. Bantō pursued learning not as a profession, but as a kind of after-work hobby. This was probably why he felt free to explore a variety of perspectives.

Scientific Perceptions Inspired by Neo-Confucianism

The senior teachers at the Kaitokudō when Bantō was a student there were Nakai Chikuzan (1730–1804) and his brother Nakai Riken (1732–1817). They were scholars of Zhu Xi neo-Confucianism. They did not, however, accept either the syncretic combination of Shintō and Zhu Xi's philosophy as advocated by Yamazaki Ansai (1619–82) and his disciple Asami Keisai (1652–1712) or the government orthodoxy of neo-Confucianism as taught by the Hayashi family. Instead, they pursued a policy of the strict textual reading. In this way they were strongly influenced by Ogyū Sorai's (1666–1728) school of "ancient learning" (*kogaku*) calling for a return to the "Six Classics" of

Confucianism and eschewing the interpretations of the later scholars such as Zhu Xi. Of the brothers, this tendency was stronger with Riken.

Asada Gōryū (1734–99), a son of a Confucian scholar in Kizuki (now part of Ōita Prefecture), physician and astronomer, left the domain to free himself from petty local affairs and to devote more time to learning. He went to the Nakai brothers for help, and began teaching at Kaitokudō as a guest lecturer. In one of his books, Riken wrote of Asada's experiments with the dissection of cadavers. In another he records his own observations through use of a microscope, showing his considerable interest in Western science.

Asada was fascinated with astronomy. He built all kinds of devices for observing heavenly bodies. He observed solar and lunar eclipses, and even foretold when they would take place. It should be noted that the new calendar the shogunate adopted in 1798 was devised by one of his students. The geographer Inō Tadataka (1745–1818), known for surveying the entire country, including Hokkaido, was a student of one of Asada's protégés.

It was under these teachers, Nakai Chikuzan and Riken and Asada Gōryū, that Yamagata Bantō studied. Because learning was a hobby he pursued after working hours, he did not produce much writing. The only work I need cite here is *Yume no shiro* (Instead of dreams), completed in 1820, which organized what he had learned during his life.

Yume no shiro consists of twelve chapters, dealing with such topics as astronomy, geography, the "age of the gods," history, institutions, economy, government, heresy, and "no soul." Deserving of greatest attention are his theories on heliocentrism discussed in the chapter on astronomy and his assertions that neither gods nor souls existed. One of his contemporaries, Kamata Ryūō (1754–

1821), also negated the existence of God, advocating a sort of theory of evolution. (He represented the intellectual lineage of the Ishida Baigan school of popular ethics, however, and was not connected with the Kaitokudō.) What is known as Confucian naturalism, if carefully thought out, would boil down to a very similar conclusion, so it is not so surprising that Yamagata Bantō should also have come up with a kind of evolutionary theory.

Neither Kamata nor Yamagata was influenced by Darwin's *Origin of Species,* which was published in 1849, about forty years after the completion of *Yume no shiro.* Moreover, Darwin put forth his theories while remaining a believer in God, but Kamata and Yamagata were consistent in their rejection of the belief in gods and spirits.

Yamagata states: "Man's birth is just like a plant sprouting from the earth, his death like its withering. His children are born the way seeds form and are dispersed. All living things are imbued with the principles of growth and decline. They grow to maturity and then decline until death, returning to the soil." A theory that the soul remains after death is wrong, argues Yamagata. "The soul exists as long as you live, but it disappears when you die."

Kamata Ryūō held very similar views. In responding to a question about the principle of the existence of the spirit (soul), he said,

> Man's life is such that the material forces (*ki*) of *yin* and *yang* [passive and active cosmic forces] gather to form a shape, which is then endowed with principle, or *ri*. Life appears when the *ki* coalesces, and death comes when it disperses. When *ki* converges, *ri* accompanies it, creating the heart. If the *ki* disperses, *ri* disappears too, erasing the heart. It is wrong to assume that the soul, or divine spirit, will exist even after death. The way man is born and dies is like the way water forms into ice and the way ice melts into water.

From where did he derive the idea that humans and other living beings were born and died in the above-mentioned manner? Behind the thinking of Kamata Ryūō was undoubtedly Ishida Baigan's teaching that "The form of a thing immediately reveals its Heart" (see *The Spirit of Japanese Capitalism,* chapter 6). But all such ideas stemmed from Zhu Xi's philosophy. Yamagata and Kamata shared similar ideas because of their common background in Zhu Xi neo-Confucianism. What, then, did Zhu Xi teach?

According to the philosophy of this twelfth-century Chinese Confucian scholar, material force (*ki;* in Chinese, *qi*) fills the universe. When it coalesces, things are created; when it disperses, they return to a gaseous state. It is the *ri* (in Chinese, *li*), or principle, that orders the coalescence or dispersal of *ki. Ri* is imminent in each and every thing. "The entirety of all things is the universal Great Ultimate, and each thing shares it." This is often likened to a moon reflected on the water in the rice field. There is only one moon, but its reflections on the water of each field create numerous images.

Man is no exception, and the *ri* is inherent in him too. Little wonder, then, that Kamata Ryūō said that human life is derived only from the combination of the material elements of water, fire, and earth. He also says:

> Remember that the air consists of such fine and minute *ki* that there is an immeasurable amount within the space as small as that of a needle's eye. The soil has myriad *ri,* so diverse kinds of plant life grow there. The water has myriad *ri,* so innumerable species of fish live in it. All things are born out of the "air" and return to the "air." People, however, think there is nothing in the air, so they cannot believe the existence of *ri.*

Because Kamata said the air was filled with *ki* and that all things would return to it, it is not surprising that he should have come up with a theory of evolution. Noting that rare morning glories had been artificially developed, he came to believe that various living things were likewise created in nature. "In recent years," he writes, "the great praises enjoyed by the morning glories of Naniwa (Osaka) have led to the artificial production of new varieties of diverse flowers and leaves, and as they spread, hundreds of types have appeared. It looks as if morning glory now has 'a thousand' different forms. From this we may assume that all trees and plants in this world derive from one kind of plant." Kamata goes on to say that animals, too, must have undergone the same process, deriving from one kind.

Human beings are no exception to this rule, he argues. Interestingly enough, Kamata regarded the process of a baby being born as the evolution of animals. "Even man is born from the mother's womb after going through the developmental changes beginning among the birds and beasts. But, because man is the most noble among all the creatures, he should be the latest in the process." This no doubt reflects his observations as a physician.

Yamagata Bantō, too, had some idea of the theory of evolution. He also advocated an idea of natural selection that was not very clear in Kamata Ryūō's work. He writes:

> The *yang* (active) force of the sun and the *yin* (passive) force of the humid earth harmonize to produce various creatures. Those who had a mouth to take in food but had no outlet for evacuation did not reproduce. Among all beings, those have survived who were equipped with such functions as make it easy for them to live. Of these, man is the best.

There is no evidence to show that Yamagata and Kamata influenced each other. Yet they shared similar ideas, clearly because of their common background in Zhu Xi philosophy. Yet, as far as I know, such ideas were not held by neo-Confucian scholars in Korea. So what gave Japanese such ideas? This is an interesting subject to study, but one I cannot pursue in detail here.

Zhu Xi neo-Confucianism is by no means a science. But Yamagata, Kamata, and other Japanese scholars of neo-Confucianism developed scientific thought. After the Meiji Restoration of 1868, when Western experts taught Darwin's theory of evolution, they expected their Japanese students to be surprised by the theory. As it turned out, they were the ones to be surprised when their students accepted the theory with no resistance at all, apparently taking it for granted. That was because, for a long time before the introduction of Darwin's ideas, the theory of evolution had been part of the intellectual mainstream in Japan. There had been no notion that man was created by God.

Yamagata and Ancestor Worship

If after death man only returned to *ki* (material force) and no soul existed, as advocated by Yamagata and Kamata, the practice of worshipping ancestral spirits would be meaningless. Confucius observed such rites with great solemnity, and did not reject the idea of "spiritual beings" (*guishen*). Was Yamagata, though a Confucian scholar, trying to deny the absolute authority of Confucius? Yamagata remarked: "We do not have to believe that all the sayings of Confucius, as recorded in the *Analects, Doctrine of the Mean, Discourses of Mencius,* are true. It is up to our wisdom which to select; we must not accept evil ideas even if they are those of Confucius. We must take whatever

257

statement is right; it does not matter who makes the statement."

This remark is impressive. It indicates an attitude of readiness to listen to anyone, even Christians from the West. And Yamagata actually did, accepting the heliocentric theory. Here let us see which of Confucius's sayings he did consider correct. A passage from the *Doctrine of the Mean* says, "All people shall attend rites, making offerings of grain and wearing formal dress. It is as if [spirit beings] were everywhere, overheard and to the right and to the left." A similar passage is also found in the *Analects:* "If you participate in a rite with sincerity, it will seem as if the deity is really present before you."

The question is, do these two passages imply that *spiritual beings really exist, but because they are not visible, it only looks as if they were present,* or *spiritual beings do not exist, but it looks as if they did?* It is hard to tell.

Yamagata took the latter interpretation. Whether you feel spiritual beings are present depends simply on your religious sensibilities. What you feel is not caused by the actual presence of spiritual beings, he argued. What, then, was his position concerning Shinto shrines and Buddhist temples, and what did he think people should do in worshipping their ancestors? What about funerals?

He said, "You should give much thought to the will of your ancestors before you decide [how to worship them]. Their souls are nonexistent, but it is right to do them the courtesy of treating them as if they existed." This idea seems to underlie the mentality of many modern Japanese, who visit shrines and temples while declaring that they "have no religion" (*mushūkyō*). Kamata Ryūō's stance was the same as Yamagata's in this respect.

Modern View of the Universe

Yamagata's theories of evolution and the nonexistence of the soul are his own conclusions, arrived at through the study of Zhu Xi neo-Confucianism. They do not represent Western influence. His understanding of heliocentrism, on the other hand, evolved under the influence of Western astronomy, as taught him by Asada Gōryū.

First, Yamagata denounces Hattori Chūyō's view of the universe based on the *Kojiki*, Japan's oldest extant chronicle (712). Hattori wrote about the universe in 1791, and his work was acclaimed by the prominent National Learning scholar Motoori Norinaga, who added it as a supplement to his famous *Kojiki Den*. Attacking Hattori's view of the universe as irrelevant and absurd, Yamagata refers to the atlas of three worlds, nine mountains, and eight seas, as taught in Buddhism, as "a figment of the imagination." He also takes up various Chinese theories about the universe, and says these are no more than the "creations of ignorant people."

Yamagata then introduces theories from Europe and says they are correct. Why? According to Yamagata,

> In European countries they do not make a map without actual survey. They invented astronomy after visiting various parts of the world, carrying out observation and conducting experiments. That is why they can navigate large ships to distant parts of the world, and make continued advances in astronomy and geography. The theories that have been maintained in India, China, and Japan are false and groundless. The theories of the Europeans are reliable.

Apparently from the time (sixteenth century) of Kamo no Arimasa (of the famous family of astronomers going back to the Heian period and, on learning Western astronomy, probably the first Japanese to become a Christian), most Japanese intellectuals ceased to believe the cosmic view as taught in Buddhism and Confucianism. Yamagata was only one of them.

Yamagata's understanding of the universe, and for that matter the understanding of his contemporaries, can be drawn from a passage from his book *Suisei kō* (A study of comets).

> The heavens are like a vast field on a dark night. A fire glows in the darkness, creating a sphere of brightness. This fire is the sun. Within its bright sphere are objects, and they receive the sun's light on one side. Six of them are big and ten small. The six are five stars and Earth. Each is a world of its own. The ten small objects are moons. One of them belongs to Earth, four to Jupiter, and five to Saturn. Each of these, too, has its world. The rest are fixed stars. The trillions of them are all suns. They are like so many fires in a dark night. Each of them has a bright sphere with "passive starts" [stars that do not emit light], each of which receives their sun's light and is a world of its own. The sun in our bright sphere is so powerful that it attracts the passive objects in the sphere, as a magnet attracts iron. Although the five stars and Earth are attracted by the sun, they have sufficient power of their own to keep away from the sun, revolving around it.

Yamagata then discusses comets and their appearance near Earth in regular intervals, saying "This is the explanation of the Westerner 'Whiston.'" Whiston was an astronomer who studied comets, following the famous Edmund Halley.

The above passage shows that Yamagata knew not only of the heliocentric theory but also the law of gravitation, and that he had learned these from the *Rekishō shinsho* (A new book on heavenly bodies), a translation, by Shizuki Tadao (1760–1806), from the Dutch version of John Keill's commentaries on Newton's *Principia*.

Yamagata Bantō felt no hesitation at all in accepting Western learning, but, as far as morality was concerned, he adhered to Confucianism. "In morals and virtues we should follow mainly the ancient sages, but it is absurd to cling to the old theories on astronomy, geography, and medicine." This idea foreshadows the slogan of nineteenth-century Japan following the opening of the country, "Western Learning, Japanese Spirit."

But Yamagata was no advocate of opening Japan's doors to the West. This may seem a bit strange, considering his intense interest in the West, not only in astronomy and medicine, but many other fields as well. In some ways, Yamagata was very conservative. As the senior clerk of a large merchant house that managed the finances of several *daimyo,* he took it for granted that the *bakuhan* (shogunate-domain) system and agrarian nationalism had to be maintained. "Japanese and Chinese should be content to be able to learn from the great Western works on astronomy, geography, and medicine while remaining at home. There is no need to sail to distant countries." Yamagata thus argued that all they had to do was to maintain the status quo and introduce necessary learning from the West.

As an advocate of the nonexistence of the soul and of the theory of heliocentrism, Yamagata said that myths were myths, even if they were an object of faith in Shinto. "We should not believe what is written in the chapter on the mythical age of gods in the *Nihon shoki* (Chronicle of Japan) (720). We should treat lightly the history from the first emperor Jinmu to just prior to the fourteenth or fifteenth emperor. The history from then onward may be relied upon." This view is roughly the same as that held by most historians today.

Was he blind, then, to the contradictions between Zhu

Xi's view of the world and the Western sciences of astronomy and medicine? He says:

> Heaven as taught in astronomy is such that it appeared before the Earth. After the Earth came man, and after man came humaneness, moral principle, propriety, wisdom, loyalty, faithfulness, filial piety, and brotherly love. Because these are all ways of controlling man, they should come after the appearance of Heaven. The origin of all of these lies in Heaven.

In short, Yamagata, like other neo-Confucian scholars, approves of Zhu Xi's idea of the principle of Heaven. But what he advocates as the principle of Heaven is an extremely modern astronomical idea. He apparently believes that the law that governs the heavenly bodies also governs man's morality—a matter of humanity, propriety, and faithfulness.

Yamagata's ideas were probably shared by teachers during the Meiji era. They would lecture on heliocentric theory with calligraphic scrolls reading "Respect Heaven, Love People," decorating their classrooms. This is basically the same attitude of most Japanese today. As a respected contemporary scholar has pointed out, however, Zhu Xi neo-Confucianism, though it seems very logical on the surface, is virtually legend. Zhu Xi believed that the same principle governed the law of Heaven, the virtues of humans, and the laws of social order. The natural, social, and inner orders are treated as the same, giving rise to the myth that as long as the society and each of its members are natural and in accord with nature then all problems can be solved.

As a thinker, Yamagata had a great deal to offer, but because he was a senior clerk in an Osaka merchant house, he was best at dealing with economic problems. He was an ardent advocate of the market economy. Thus, he believed that the economy controlled by the shogunate and the domains would suffer more than prosper. In 1782 to 1787 many domains in Japan suffered severe food shortages (the Tenmei famines) resulting from crop failure. Yamagata believed that the misery in hardest-hit areas like the Nanbu domain was a man-made disaster, brought about by insufficient distribution systems. He highly praised the functions of the Dōjima Rice Market in Osaka and proposed that rice markets be set up in Edo and other big cities, with Dōjima as the center.

A rationalist, he also hit on the idea of issuing "rice coupons" to extricate the Sendai domain from its fiscal crisis. His method was this: issuing rice coupons to obtain funds with which to purchase rice; reserving some of the rice for use in exchange for coupons, and selling the rest in Osaka to obtain silver; and depositing the silver with money changers (*ryōgaeshō*), and using the interest from this to pay back the domain's loans.

He tried to view everything, from the economy to astronomy, in a rational manner. These attitudes held by Yamagata, Tominaga, and many others in the Tokugawa era formed the basis of modern Japanese thinking.